DREAMS & RECIPES 1904 -1914

Viola Dono

Analogy Press
Belfast

Viola Dono was born in Enniskillen, Northern Ireland in 1968

Dreams & Recipes 1904 - 1914

First published in the UK in 2014 by Analogy Press

Copyright © Viola Dono 2014

This work is subject to copyright protection and in accordance with the Copyright Design and Patents Act 1988, the following are prohibited acts, where our permission has not been granted or exclusions under the Act do not apply: (i) copying; (ii) issuing, lending, showing or communicating copies to the public; and (iii) reproducing, modifying or adapting the content in whole or in part. Any permitted copying or reproduction shall acknowledge us as follows: "Reproduced with kind permission of Analogy Press and Viola Dono" If you wish to obtain our permission please email sales@analogypress.com

ISBN-13: 978-0993095917

Cover reproduced from 'New York' painted in 1911 by George Bellows (1882 - 1925).

Credit - Painting in the collection of Mr and Mrs Paul Mellon.

To the lovers, the haters,
the users, the losers,
the holy, the lowly,
the Glory Hole Steward.
To the sinners, the winners,
the child and the grown-up,
the racer, the chaser,
the Crane Operator,
the mason, the stoker,
the draughtsman, the poker,
the deflated, the elated,
the Druid, the Faust.
To the caster, the trimmer,
the migrant, the spinner,
the flattered, the shattered,
the musician by night,
To the farmer, the charmer,
the peaceful disarmer,
the butcher, the baker,
the Mysterious Pudding Maker...

For Daniel

Based on several intertwining true stories...

Introduction

I grew up in Northern Ireland in an apolitical family of bakers, establishing my own wholesale bakery business in the summer of 1990. We baked Irish fruit cakes, breads and tray bakes, supplying customers right across the island of Ireland and mainland UK. I loved every chance to get a day out from the bakery, meeting new customers in Belfast, some days Dublin, and many country villages and towns in between. Heading home into molten western sunsets, through villages with the fragrance of smouldering turf hanging softly in the air, my homeland seemed enchanting and magical in those misty twilight evenings. After 20 years of driving down the same roads, a series of life-changing and ultimately serendipitous events led to me heading down other trails and pathways, though still primarily on the track of food.

While compiling a recipe book from my years as a baker, I became spellbound by some old recipes handed down to me from the beginning of the 20th century. Recipes which I had passed over in the headlong rush of life and my own mercantile way of doing things, were asking me to slow down and take a closer look. I stopped in my tracks and the pulse of the past took over. I quickly realised that the scale and richness of the recipes from those first years of the 20th century, and the characters and spirit of the people's names attached to them, demanded a book singularly devoted to them.

The book was born with a life of its own, each day leading me deeper down unexpected and remarkable paths. My own recipes could wait another day, something was telling me now was the time to share these tales from my beloved homeland.

The many colourful characters from 100 years ago tell us a lot about the quite recent past. It was a time of great social change around the world. Books were only beginning to be within the reach of working class folk in the last few decades of the 19th century. In the early 1800s barely half the population were literate; mass literacy was feared by politicians and religious leaders alike and heavy taxes were imposed on newspapers and pamphlets with the Stamp Act of 1712, an act which stayed in force until 1855. Despite all this nearly everyone could read and write by the 1890s.

And so it was; as I stared at recipes dated 1903, 1907 and 1913 written by local people, many with names attached, I felt an overwhelming desire to delve into my past. I was holding in my hands some of the very early records of recipes chronicled by people who lived 'just down the road from me' one hundred years ago.

So many food books take it upon themselves to paint a picture of a land that got by on dull, tasteless food, until some big gun celebrity chef came along to teach us all how to cook. Such storylines bewildered me as I recalled the amazing tastes and flavours of my childhood at Mum's table and both my Grandmas' too. Fresh catch from unpolluted waters teeming with fish, and truly organic vegetables cultivated in the lush greenery of a temperate climate, have always tasted undeniably amazing.

Fresh cream, homemade butter, free range eggs and honey; it would be hard to know where you could go wrong really. Not to mention the vast array of wonderful breads, farls, pancakes, pies and cakes which were baked each day with the most basic of kitchen tools.

A focused look dispelled some common myths of what food was really like here. Perhaps the biggest surprise I got was when it dawned on me that my Belfast recipes dated around 1907 included so many which called for the use of an oven. Traditional pictures of my homeland at that time always portray a kitchen with a large fireplace, griddle and a black cooking pot, without an oven in sight. Yes, this was true for many people, but by all accounts in my books, there were more than just a few houses with ovens for baking in by 1907. The names beside the contributed recipes proved that it wasn't just the very wealthy who were baking sponge cakes back then either. Years earlier, over in the west just outside the little village of Kesh, Dr Lombe Atthill (1827 – 1910) wrote in his memoirs 'Even wheat was grown, and a sufficient quantity ground by means of a hand- mill placed in a loft, to supply wholemeal to make brown bread. Flour, however, had to be bought. The week's supply of bread was baked once a week in a brick oven.' His childhood memories of Christmas look back on, 'a splendid plum pudding as big as a small haycock; this would be carried in all aflame. There were mince pies, too, home-made cakes, etc., and for us youngsters a bottle of home-made gooseberry wine'.

'Flame, The Gasworks Museum of Ireland' in Carrickfergus, County Antrim, Northern Ireland has an amazing collection of nineteenth & twentieth century domestic and commercial gas appliances such as cookers, fires, heaters, washing machines, fridges, irons, pokers, and lights (some of which are still working). Records there show that in 1904 there were 9562 cookers in Belfast, with a grand total of 14 292 in Dublin. By 1914 these figures had risen to 24 477 cookers in Belfast, whilst Dublin had a whopping 48 109. There certainly was a lot of oven baking and cooking going on. Gas and electric ovens reached rural areas much later in the 20th century. It wasn't until 1943 that Northern Ireland's first electricity power station was commissioned at Ballylumford in County Antrim. The Electricity Supply Act in 1955 began the process of rural electrification, bringing welcome light and power to provincial houses back then.

So recipes aren't just about food. They tell another story too. I wonder what they will tell you… Let me take you on a journey right into the centre of homes, hearts and lives here. Together we'll peek through some Edwardian kitchen windows as seen through the pages of the past from 1904 – 1914.

The main part of the book is told as an epistolary account through a series of letters, and is based on several intertwining true stories. It's a novella and recipe book combined, communicated mainly through two young girls over a ten year period as they are growing up.

I have used the writing genre known as 'faction', changing some names, stories and locations of members of my own family, and veiling them to a certain degree in fictional disguise for privacy's sake. (The Oxford English Dictionary describes the genre of 'faction' as 'A literary and cinematic genre in which fictional narrative is developed from a basis of real events or characters'.) Occasionally the letters are Bakhtinian in style, carrying the taste of other voices and the heart of other feelings as they speak.

The dialogues concerning Henry Cust, Lady Londonderry, Lady Whitla, the Ewarts and other well-known local characters are direct from real life events. The excerpts from contemporary writers of the day including W.B. Yeats and Katharine Tynan are all from old family books. The recipes are credited to the original people who wrote them out. Any recipes which have neither name nor initial are my own family recipes from the same time period. The recipes have annotations to the imperial amounts in grams and American cups, and vice versa towards the end of the book with the American recipes which my grandmother used as a young bride. It is important to note that an American cup is much larger than those cups which would have been used for measuring in Irish and British kitchens. An American cup holds 236 millitres of liquid.

Emigration is a big part of my family history. My maternal Granda's great grandfather Daniel McMorris left Ireland in 1846, one of the worst years of the Great Famine. He died one year later in Philadelphia, aged just 57. My Granda's great grandfather's sister was called Martha McMorris. She was born around 1787 in a place called Donagheady in Co Tyrone. In 1816 she married William Cooper in Co. Tyrone. They are mentioned in *'Jefferson County, Pennsylvania - Her Pioneers and People, Vol. II,'* by Dr. William James McKnight, published in 1917 by J.H. Beers & Company, Chicago, page 654.

'William Cooper brought his family from County Tyrone, Ireland, in 1823, landing after a voyage of thirteen weeks. They drove to Valentine's Furnace, in Center County, PA., where he found work about the furnaces. Three years later they came to western Pennsylvania, journeying by wagon to Luther burg and with ox-sled to the Beechwoods, in Washington Township, Jefferson County, where they arrived in February, 1826. He located a forest tract of 200 acres near the centre of the Beechwoods, at what later became known as Rockdale Mills. Only two or three settlers had preceded them, the Osborn's, Keys, McGee's and MacIntoshes being their nearest neighbours. The usual log cabin was constructed and provided with home-made furniture'... 'William Cooper spent the remainder of his life making improvements and helping to enhance civilization. He cleared part of the farm later owned by his son James Cooper, and there died in February, 1868, at the age of eighty years, his wife, Martha (McMorris) Cooper, surviving until 1871... William Cooper was long remembered as a typical Irishman, quick-witted and ever ready with a sharp answer, his humour and friendly nature making him popular in a wide circle'

My Mum's father grew up in County Fermanagh in a family of 16, nearly half of whom emigrated to Canada (Montreal), USA (Los Angeles), and Australia. Granda himself left Fermanagh as a young man to work as a carpenter on the railways in Belfast. Mum's grandmother, Eliza Jane, left County Armagh for New York at the age of 12. When her mother became ill she returned towards the end of her teenage years, never forgetting her formative years in 'The States'.

My Dad's mother Sophia left Cavan as a young woman, to earn a living in America. She worked hard and landed a position in a millionaire household, good times which she spoke affectionately of for the rest of her life. While there she met my Granda, a young Fermanagh man, fell head over heels in love, and they were married in Brooklyn, New York. Granda was a farmer at heart, and after a while he wrote home to his brother asking him to look out for a place for them back in Fermanagh. A suitable farm was found and Granda sent on the money. In her trunk, Granny brought back a little piece of the States – a cookery book entitled *'The Way to a Man's Heart'* by Lizzie Black Kander. My letters finish up with a selection of recipes from that very book. An extensive American avant-garde answer to the English Mrs Beeton, I selected many of its recipes with the simple guidance of Granny's well thumbed pages, which made it easy to tell which recipes she baked in her Fermanagh kitchen over and over again.

Many a time, flying in home circling cirrus clouds, Walt Whitman's words resound in my head,

'Will you seek afar off? You surely come back at last,
In things best known to you finding the best, or as good as the best;
In folks nearest to you finding the sweetest, strongest, and lovingest;
Happiness, knowledge not in another place, but this place –
Not for another hour but this hour.'

We've still got little turf scented villages here, and houses with the tick- tock of the mantelpiece clock in the 'good room'. We've still got summer hedges of honeysuckle, fields of golden buttercups, and we've still got dozens of gloriously unspoilt, half deserted beaches right along our breath-taking coastline. We still make great brown soda bread here, and teabreads and sponge cakes filled with fresh fruit and cream. We still make summer jams, pancakes, puddings and pies, traybakes, tartlets, crumbles and buns shaped like butterflies ... and still dream of peace in our lullabies.

April 2014

Ode

We are the music-makers,
And we are the dreamers of dreams,
Wandering by lone sea-breakers,
And sitting by desolate streams;
World losers and world forsakers,
On whom the pale moon gleams:
Yet we are the movers and shakers
Of the world for ever, it seems.
With wonderful deathless ditties
We build up the world's great cities,
And out of a fabulous story
We fashion an empire's glory:
One man with a dream, at pleasure,
Shall go forth and conquer a crown;
And three with a new song's measure
Can trample an empire down.
We, in the ages lying
In the buried past of the earth,
Built Nineveh with our sighing,
And Babel itself with our mirth;
And o'erthrew them with prophesying
To the old of the new world's worth;
For each age is a dream that is dying,
Or one that is coming to birth.

Arthur William Edgar O'Shaughnessy
(14 March 1844 – 30 January 1881)

Narrator: The Immigration and Naturalisation Service of the US records for 1901 -1910 gave immigration figures from Ireland as 339, 065. Ireland was not alone in losing large numbers of her people . Even greater numbers emigrated to the US in these years from Italy with 2 045, 266, Austria and Hungary with a combined total of 2 145,566, Russia 1, 597 300, Germany 341, 498 and England 388, 017. Significant numbers came too from Belgium, Bulgaria, Denmark, France, Scotland, Wales, Greece, The Netherlands, Norway, Portugal, Romania, Spain, Sweden, Switzerland, Turkey, China and Japan. The total number of individuals who emigrated to America in this first decade of the twentieth century was just under 9 million. Each one was someone's daughter, son, brother, sister, mother or father. Each one had a dream.

Sunday May 22nd 1904
Cavan

Dear Eliza,

How are you all in Belfast? I hope you're all keeping well. We are so very lonesome here. Sophia has just left for The States and Mam is broken hearted. She's gone to work as a domestic servant in Brooklyn, New York. Mr Porter from The Royal Arms Hotel in Omagh sorted it all out for her. He's the man everyone goes to when they make their mind up to leave. Sophia left me his leaflet in case I should decide to go too someday. It was like a wake house here the night before she left. Mam was inconsolable. I've been dreaming of going myself but I really don't know if I could put Mam through that again.

"John G.R. Porter, General Emigration and Booking Agent, Royal Arms Hotel, Omagh. Tickets issued to all parts of United States and Canada, Australia, New Zealand, South Africa etcetera at lowest emigrant fares.

Agent for The Allan Line, Dominion Line, White Star Line and Inman Line to America, The Orient and P & O Lines to Australia and New Zealand, Castle Line to South Africa.

Special advantages offered to Canadian emigrants. Female domestic servants in great demand. Parties going to Canada will find it to their advantage to book through me, and I will be happy to furnish them with Letters of Introduction to friends in Montreal, who will render them valuable assistance in securing good situations. Intending emigrants supplied gratis with every necessary information, pamphlets, dates of sailing, etcetera, on application. John G.R. Porter, general Emigration Office, Omagh. American money exchanged"

Every day I read it Eliza, it puts a shiver through me. It's like Sophia has died. Mam is so afraid that she'll never see her daughter again.

Just before she left, John's sister Miss Porter handed Sophia her famous dessert recipe for Pineapple Pudding. It's the one she serves to her guests in the hotel ,and she told Sophia it could be useful to her in The States.

Pineapple Pudding
By Miss Porter, Royal Arms Hotel, Omagh,
Co. Tyrone

Ingredients:
- 55g / 2 oz / 1/2 stick butter
- 55g / 2 oz / 2/5 cup cornflour / cornstarch
- ½ Imperial pint / 284 ml / 1.2 cups milk
- 55g / 2 oz / 1/4 cup caster sugar
- 2 eggs, separated (reserve whites for meringue topping)
- 200g / 7 oz / 1 cup / small tin of pineapple chunks, drained – reserve the pineapple juice to thin out pudding batter

For meringue topping
- 110g / 4 oz / 1/2 cup caster sugar

Method:
1. Melt the butter in a saucepan.
2. Add the cornflour / cornstarch and milk, and mix till smooth.
3. Add the yolks of the eggs, sugar, and 60 ml/ 1/4 cup of the pineapple juice. Simmer until starting to thicken – if too thick add a little more pineapple juice.
4. Transfer to a greased ovenproof bowl and pour over the drained pineapple chunks.
5. Bake at 170 C / 325F / Gas Mark 3 for 30 minutes.
6. Reduce the oven heat to 150C / 300F /Gas Mark 2.
7. Whisk reserved egg whites until they form peaks, then add in the meringue topping caster sugar and whisk again to form stiff peaks. Pile on top of the pudding and swirl with a spoon to form a nice topping.
8. Return to oven and bake for 10 – 15 minutes until the meringue is a light golden colour.

I like it best still warm from the oven Eliza. I hope Sophia is getting on okay. It seems like forever waiting on a letter from her. Michael's talking about going to New Zealand and Frank heard Mrs Murphy boasting the other day that her sons are making their fortune in England. It will break Mam's heart if any more of us go. Let me know what you think of the pudding Eliza. I look forward to hearing from you soon,
        Love,
        Lillie

Narrator: The Royal Arms Hotel was centrally located on Omagh High Street, and was a popular inn since the latter part of the 18th century. The hotel finally closed it's doors at the end of the 20th century, after a bomb was planted close to it on the 15th of August 1998. The 29th person to die from his injuries 3 weeks after the bomb went off was a good friend and mentor to the author. Sean McGrath was born in this same street 61 years before the explosion that fatally injured him. He was a businessman and bakery owner, supplying a large customer base which included Harrods of Knightsbridge, London, before he 'retired' to advise and guide others in the bakery trade. As the news of his passing filtered through, a local paper carried the heartfelt front page headline, 'A Heavenly Man'.

Monday September 12th, 1904
Belfast

Dear Lillie,

I hope you're keeping well. Have you heard from Sophia yet? I think she's very brave. We're all doing just fine and really loved the pineapple pudding. Miss Porter's hotel guests must really love it too. I called in with Auntie Annie last week to give her the recipe and I bumped into the new lodger in the porchway. Oh Lillie, he's the most handsome man I've ever seen. He's nearly six feet tall, with lovely dark hair and the most adorable brown eyes. He smiled at me and I just fell to pieces. I was so nervous I didn't know what to say until Aunt Annie came out and introduced us. His name is Tommy and he works down in Queen's Island in the shipyard.

Aunt Annie says he just thinks of work all the time. She says the Andrews family are strict Unitarians, and Tommy's mother promised her sons a big reward if they didn't touch cigarettes or drink before they were 21 years old. She says he's advancing at work every day. Apparently his mother is a sister of Lord Pirrie, who is the owner of the shipyard. I wonder has he any time in his life for romance. He's so handsome I'd just like to get lost in his arms Lillie. He just seems like the kind of person you could trust with your life forever.

Last Saturday Mother took us to see a wedding in Ballysillan. It was one of the prettiest I've ever seen. Violet Villiers Ewart, from the linen merchant family, got married to Mr Gerald Lutwyche. He comes from Beckenham in London. The bridal party walked from the house to the church and most of Ligoniel came out to watch. The children from St. Mark's school stood at the entrance to the church and threw flowers in the path of the bride. Violet's uncle Sir William Ewart gave her away. I stood there dreaming it was I who was getting married, and Tommy was my man.

The bride's dress was white crepe-de-chine, trimmed with point lace, and the bodice was drawn up into a deep swathed belt. The Court train was made from lovely satin, edged with tulle and lilies-of-the-valley. Her veil of embroidered tulle was fastened by a coronet of orange blossoms, shamrocks and white heather. The bridesmaids wore dresses made of India muslin and long lace mittens. They had coronets of white heather and shamrocks and the little train bearers had these too – they looked so lovely in their Empire dresses with waistbands of white satin.

Violet's mother, Mrs Ewart, wore a lovely gown of black lace and chiffon over white silk and a toque made of black chiffon with ostrich plumes. She carried a bouquet of crimson roses. Lillie, you should have seen Lady Jaffe – she's from The States and is married to Sir Otto Jaffe; he was born in Hamburg and is Belfast's Lord Mayor again this year. She was wearing a beautiful grey dress with a bodice of cream satin and point lace. Her toque was made of satin and trimmed with velvet and roses, and she wore a beautiful grey feather stole.

Oh Lillie, Mother talks most days of the years she worked in New York as a nurse maid. She learnt so many grand ways out there in just under six years. Can you believe she was only twelve years old when she went out to Mr Chapman and his family in New York? She was so small looking when she arrived that he sent her to school with his own children for half a term. When Mr Chapman saw how pretty Mother was he warned her to walk well out on the pavements away from the buildings in case any bad men dragged her in off the street. I think she is very brave and strong. She only came home because Grandmother was ill, but then again if she hadn't returned, she wouldn't have met Father and I wouldn't be here now to write this!

Before I bumped into Tommy the other day I had been thinking that I should like to go to The States too…what do you think Lillie?

Please write back soon,
    Eliza

PS Aunt Annie says Tommy sits up until 11 o' clock every night working at his desk, and is up at 10 to 5 each morning to be at the yard at 6!

Do you know, one of his favourite poems is Henry Van Dyke's "Work"… he has brought a framed picture of it to hang up in his room. Grandma says it's a good way to think if you're a shipbuilder and not short of a pound like Tommy. If you're working at slaughtering speed in one of the factories and barely making enough to keep food on the table, then it's not the kind of poem that's going to make you feel any better at the end of the day. She says the well-filled belly has little understanding of the empty. Then again, Henry

Van Dyke is from The States, and couldn't have been thinking of the factorries in Belfast when he wrote this.

Work
By Henry Van Dyke

Let me but do my work from day to day,
In field or forest, at the desk or loom,
In roaring market-place or tranquil room;
Let me but find it in my heart to say,
When vagrant wishes beckon me astray,
"This is my work; my blessing, not my doom;
"Of all who live, I am the one by whom
"This work can best be done in the right way."

Then shall I see it not too great, nor small,
To suit my spirit and to prove my powers;
Then shall I cheerful greet the labouring hours,
And cheerful turn, when the long shadows fall
At eventide, to play and love and rest,
Because I know for me my work is best.

Narrator: In his bachelor years in the early 1900s, Thomas Andrews, chief designer of RMS Titanic, boarded at 11 Wellington Place, Belfast, County Antrim at the home of sisters Jane and Hannah Scott. Like Andrews, the sisters were both devout Unitarians. Hannah was a teacher and her sister Jane a dressmaker. They employed domestic servant Hannah Callan to look after the household. Thomas Andrews hung a framed picture of Van Dyke's poem 'Work' in his room.
11 Wellington Place is right in the heart of Belfast city centre and today is the site of a contemporary restaurant called 'The Maze'.

Before I go...here is Grandmother's recipe for pancakes. She taught Mother and Aunt Annie how to make these.

Grandmother's Pancakes

Ingredients:
- Plain flour - 8 oz / 225g / 2 cups
- Butter or margarine - 2 oz / 55g / 1/2 stick
- Caster sugar - 2 oz / 55g /1/4 cup
- Bicarbonate of Soda - 1/2 level teaspoon
- Baking Powder - 1 level teaspoon
- Salt - a pinch
- Egg - 1
- Buttermilk - 1/2 pint (approx.) / 284 ml / 1.2 cups
- Apples - a fresh slice for each pancake (optional)

Method:
1. Sieve dry ingredients and rub in margarine.
2. Drop in egg and a little of the buttermilk. Mix quickly to a smooth paste and add enough buttermilk to make a thick batter.
3. Grease a low to medium heated griddle or pan and drop batter to form pancake size required. Top each pancake with a slice of apple.
4. When base is set and bubbles rise, turn pancake and cook to a golden brown.

She keeps the pancakes hot in a folded cloth while she finishes making the batch. I hope you like them,

Eliza

Tuesday November 1st 1904
Cavan

Dear Eliza,

Thank you for your letter in September. I read it over and over again. You described the wedding so well I almost imagined I was there. Eliza, I hope you don't mind me saying - don't you go falling in love with someone above your station. A man like that will only marry someone on his own la-di-da level for sure, except maybe in your dreams Eliza.

Sophia has written to us for the first time since she left. She's awfully busy in her new house with so many things. She has chambermaid duties, wash day tasks, clearing up after meals, polishing silver, sweeping out rooms and so many other things, she just sinks into her bed exhausted every night. She sleeps in a tiny little room near the kitchen. She wants Mam to send out recipes, as she's expected to help the cook after she has settled in. Everything is measured in cups in The States, and Sophia says they're not anything like the cups we drink out of here. An American cup is a special measure that holds 236 ml of liquid. Mam has found a tin mug that's the same size and she's going to try and convert her pounds and ounces recipes for Sophia before she sends them out.

Sophia is paid six dollars a week. I think that's very good as she doesn't have to pay for her food and lodgings. Sophia says Mrs Logan told her she can have a sweetheart visit in the evenings, but Sophia is so tired at the moment it's all she can do to get through the working day!

The pancakes are perfect. Thanks for the recipe. Mam says if I want to go and work in a big house I should keep a book with all my recipes written in it. We could share recipes with each other in our letters if you'd like to. I really will watch Mam extra carefully when she's making everything from now on.

Father is fattening up the turkeys for Christmas - one for ourselves and the rest for sale at the market. Mam boils up all the old rough potatoes, pounds them, then mixes them with poultry meal and feeds it to the turkeys. Father gives them raw cabbage to stop them from pecking at each other. Grandma always cooked goose at Christmas but I would rather have turkey. Do you like goose Eliza?

Here is Aunt Minnie's Christmas pudding recipe from when she worked in that big house in Dublin. I love to slice a little bit off and eat it cold like cake. It's not like those old suet ones at all.

Christmas Pudding

Ingredients:
- 110g / 4 oz / 2 cups fine breadcrumbs (brown or white)
- 225g / 8 oz /1 cup hot water
- 300g / 11 oz / 1.5 cups brown sugar
- 40g / 1.5 oz / 1/3 cup ground almonds
- 335g / 12 oz / 3 sticks butter (melted)
- 6 eggs
- 75g / 3 oz / 1/4 cup treacle
- 1 teaspoon lemon essence
- 225g / 8 oz / 2 cups all-purpose plain flour
- 1 teaspoon ground mixed spice
- about half a teaspoon freshly grated nutmeg
- 900g / 2 lb. 2 oz / 7.5 cups sultanas
- 335g / 12oz / 2 cups currants
- 55g / 2oz / 1/2 cup finely chopped candied peel
- 55g / 2 oz / 1/2 cup preserved ginger in sugar syrup, drained and finely chopped
- 75g / 3 oz / 1/2 cup glacé cherries
- 75g / 3 oz / 3/4 cup flaked almonds
- 75g /3 oz / 1/2 cup walnuts, roughly chopped

Method:
1. Measure out the sultanas and currants into a bowl and cover them with warm water. Leave to steep for half an hour, then drain well, discarding the water.
2. In another bowl mix the breadcrumbs with the measured out amount of hot water.
3. Add the brown sugar, ground almonds, and melted butter and mix all together well.

4. Beat the eggs and add these to the breadcrumb mixture along with the treacle and lemon essence and mix all together until combined.
5. Weigh out the flour and blend in the mixed spice and nutmeg. Add these to the breadcrumb and egg mixture.
6. Next add the fruits, ginger and nuts and mix together well.
7. Put into 3 well-greased 2 pint / 1.125 pudding basins, cover and set in the oven in a deep pan filled with water.
8. Bake between 150 – 170C / 300 -325F / Gas Mark 2 -3 for about 1 hour and 45 minutes.

Every day now I think about leaving to work in the States. Did you know there were even women boxing in the Olympics there this year? Michael says they should catch themselves on, but Aunt Minnie says it's the land where dreams really can come true. Write soon please Eliza.

Love,
Lillie

Narrator: Work was hard as an immigrant domestic servant in a new country, but domestic workers were in great demand. The live-in arrangement had the advantage of providing a sort of 'home' base for Irish country girls in a strange new city, in an unfamiliar new land.
The United States 'Report of the Industrial Commission on the Relations of Capital and Labor Volume VII' (United States 1901, p33) talks of the necessity of a living wage. 'A wage sufficient to maintain the worker and those dependant on him in a degree of comfort commensurate with his economic and social surroundings, as one of the most important contentions of labour'. The report stated that Ireland and much of Continental Europe did not enjoy the same wages and conditions as Americans, but believed that wages in England were on a par with America at that time. The 'living wage' is still an elusive dream for many hard-working employees around the world today, more than a century after this report highlighted the issue.

Wednesday 14th December 1904
Belfast

Dear Lillie,

      I think it's a great idea to keep a little book with our best recipes in it. Your Aunt Minnie's Christmas pudding recipe is just perfect. Mother has made half a dozen of them and is giving away four as Christmas presents.

Sam and I have been out climbing trees picking all the holly we can find with red berries on. We have put some above every picture in the house. I'm dreaming of Christmas dinner already. We usually have goose to eat. Father killed it yesterday and plucked it while it was still warm. He has hung it up in the shed next to the dairy. Hopefully none of the cats will get at it there. Last Christmas one of them got into the outhouse where the goose was hanging and ate the whole breast of one side of it! We didn't notice until Christmas Eve. Mother had to clean it up and cook it anyhow. She just got her big packing needle out and sewed the goose up to keep the stuffing in.

Father has just came in and thrown a big powder dry log on the turf fire. The flames are blazing and flickering over the red-berried holly and ivy that Sam and I put up. Mother has put up a little bunch of mistletoe to kiss Father under when we are all tucked up in bed. I love to listen to them whispering and laughing when they think we're fast asleep.

Father has bought Mother a beautiful pair of deerskin gloves for Christmas. She likes to wear gloves in public as they hide how worn her hands look from all the years of work and laundry. Mother has hidden a new fountain pen in the dresser for Father. She hopes it will make him enjoy writing more. He isn't very good at it and writes very slowly. She's been saving up for ages from her lace-making money.

Here is our favourite Christmas Crumble recipe. I am going to curl up to sleep now and dream of Christmas.

Christmas Crumble

Ingredients:
- 405g / 15 oz/ about 6 or 7 medium apples, peeled, cored and cut into chunks
- 405g / 15 oz /1.5 cups sweet mincemeat

Topping:
- 225g / 8 oz / 2 cups plain flour
- 85g / 3 oz / 1/2 cup light brown sugar
- 55g / 2 oz / 1/2 stick butter
- 1 level teaspoon ground cloves

Method:
1. Mix apples and sweet mincemeat well together and put into an oven-proof dish approximate size 22.5 cm / 9 inch diameter and 7.5 cm /3 inches deep.

To make the topping:
1. Chop butter into small pieces and rub into the flour until it resembles fine breadcrumbs.
2. Mix in the light brown sugar and ground cloves.
3. Sprinkle across top of the fruit and bake slowly at 180C / 350F / Gas Mark 4 for 45 minutes – 1 hour. Serve warm.

Have a lovely Christmas Lillie,
Love,
Eliza

Narrator: Though many married women's place was seen as being in the home in Ireland, by the late 1890s home-industry such as lace-making, poultry-keeping and embroidery and dress-making often brought in 50% or more of the household income. (Barclay 2012, p573).

Wednesday 8th February 1905
Cavan

Dear Eliza,

The last crumbs of Christmas have gone, and Mam is up the walls here about Frank. He's been going through an awful time at school, and says he can't bear it another day. Eliza, my brother is so brainy, but can just never seem to do anything right at school. He's just given up and won't talk about it anymore. Father says Frank is old enough to work with him on the road contracts now, so that's what he's going to do. Mam says it's so unfair that one bad master can completely and utterly destroy a child's education. Aunt Margaret was here for Christmas and talked to father a lot about it. She says the Irish obstetrician Dr Lombe Atthill, who grew up in Ardess just outside Kesh in County Fermanagh, is writing down his life story now that he has reached his retirement. She says he's blowing the lid of what life has been really like here and he's a man who really calls a spade a spade. He says he has some terrible early memories that he feels moved to write down before he dies.

Dr Atthill's father came to Ireland in 1798 to work as chaplain to the bishop of Clogher. He says that it was only in the larger towns that any means of educating the poor existed, other than that afforded by the 'Hedge School Masters,' a class of men themselves little above actual beggary, who wandered about the country, imparting their own scanty knowledge to the children of those who would supply them with food and afford them a lodging.

Isn't it so sad that a land of scholars, where wealthy families in Europe sent their children to be educated over a thousand years ago, should be reduced to this state of affairs by the 19th century? Did you know Eliza that it was the Irish who invented word spacing sometime around the eighth century AD? Where would the world be without us!

Tryingtodecipherwhatonearttheverythingsaidwouldbesopeskywouldntit?

When Dr Atthill was old enough, his parents sent him off to Maidstone in Kent to grammar school for 2 years; days that he remembers with fondness. He says that he learnt from his master, Mr. Harrison, the true meaning of fairness. One day during a squabble between him and his pals with some bigger boys, they inadvertently smashed many small diamond shaped panes of glass whilst throwing cabbage stalks in an attempt to defend themselves. When the master asked for each boy to say how many panes they had shattered, Lombe admitted that he had personally smashed a dozen or so of them himself. The other boys each said they had smashed only one or two. The master called Lombe to his office, congratulated him on his honesty, handed him half a crown, and invited him to dinner. Lombe later used the half crown to purchase a fishing rod.

Aunt Margaret says he is highly regarded in Dublin where he was Master of the Rotunda Hospital and President of the Royal College of Physicians of Ireland. I wonder would Dr Atthill have grown up into a different man had he not met Mr Harrison in Maidstone when he was in his most formative years? He says he came harshly back to reality on his return to a badly run school here, where he was pronounced idle, caned and "kept in" frequently. He eventually refused to attend there, all was so horrible.

Aunt Margaret says the doctor remembers as a young adult, smelling the stench of potatoes rotting in the fields at the outset of The Great Famine. He blames starvation on the lack of proper roads, in Fermanagh and the rest of Ireland, to transport the available food to the local people. He says there was such a lot of waste and mismanagement of funds, and if the government had let plans for the building of railways go ahead, a huge number of lives would have been saved. It's hard to believe the government spent over seven times as much money sending people to fight in the Crimean War just a few years after the famine here.

We're baking Aunt Margaret's recipe for Oaten Apple for supper tonight. I hope you like it! Looking forward to hearing from you soon.

Love,
Lillie

Oaten Apple

Ingredients:
- 110g /4 oz / 1 cup porridge oats
- 140g / 5 oz / 1.25 cups plain flour
- a good pinch of bicarbonate of soda
- a good pinch of salt
- 110 g / 4 oz / 1/2 cup light brown sugar
- 110 g / 4 oz / 1/2 cup melted butter
- 365 g /13 oz / 3 packed cups sliced eating apples
- 1/4 level teaspoon ground cinnamon
- 2 tablespoons caster sugar

Method:
1. Preheat oven to 180C / 350F / Gas Mark 4.
2. Put oats, flour, bicarbonate of soda, salt, light brown sugar, and melted butter in a large bowl and mix well.
3. Press half of this mixture evenly across the bottom of a 21cm / 8 inch loose bottomed circular cake tin. Toss the sliced apples, ground cinnamon, and caster sugar together in a bowl. Lay these evenly across the base.
4. Sprinkle the rest of the oat mixture evenly over the top, flattening it down a little. Bake for approximately 45 minutes until a nice golden colour.

Narrator: Dr. Attill died suddenly in 1910 and his memoirs were posthumously published the following year by The Religious Tract Society and Analogy Press (with glossary 2015). His accounts of 19th century life are frank and veracious, and make a valuable contribution to Irish history of the time. His despair at the treatment he received at the prestigious Royal School in Enniskillen, (the same school Oscar Wilde boarded at from 1864 - 1872, and Samuel Beckett attended from 1920 -1923) contrast greatly to his happy days at an English school in Maidstone, Kent. Chapters on the Irish Famine, the Irish railways, life in the medical profession and the pain of emigration, vividly describe these turbulent years in this rare insight which Dr. Attill so conscientiously recorded for future generations.

Tuesday 25th April 1905
Belfast

Dear Lillie,

It's good that Dr Atthill is going to write down what goes on here. Grandma says it's hard for our writers because they feel duty bound to tell things as they are and many people don't like hearing the truth. Dr Atthill is known across the land as the best obstetrician and gynaecologist there has ever been.

Spring is finally here. The grass is getting greener and the corncrake and cuckoo have arrived. I wonder is Sophia missing Ireland. Mother says she missed our summertime so much when she was in the States – she dreamed of the late sunsets, meadow buttercups and red clover, and carpets of bell heather and bluebells everywhere. I love when the field behind our house fills up with daisies and buttercups.

Mother says winters are so cold in New York. I love the light evenings now and especially in a few weeks' time when it will be bright until nearly midnight. She says it gets dark much earlier in summer evenings in New York and when she went away she dreamt of our summer celtic twilights. Even when the darkness sneaks in after sundown it never seems to get pitch black in summertime here.

We've been baking constantly over the last few weeks. Every time I bake I imagine Tommy and I are married and I'm baking everything for him coming in every night after work. I'm trying to dream up excuses to drop by Aunt Annie's place but I lose courage at the last minute.

Here are two more recipes for our collection. The fadge recipe is really good for anyone who can't take milk or buttermilk. It's a really old recipe. Father says he prefers it to cake anyday.

We've gathered up a lot of flour bags in the last few months, ready to try out our new sewing machine. Sam has made a lovely wooden roller and we're going to sew sheets together to make a long towel cloth for the scullery.

Please write soon,

                  Eliza

Sultana Scones

Ingredients:
- 335 g / 12 oz / 3 cups plain flour
- 2 x 15 ml tablespoons caster sugar
- 1 beaten egg
- 8 fl oz / 225 g soured cream
- 140g / 5 oz / 1 cup sultanas
- 1.5 level teaspoons baking powder
- 1/8 teaspoon bicarbonate of soda
- 1/4 teaspoon salt

Method:
1. Preheat oven to 190C/ 375F / Gas Mark 5. Grease and flour a baking tin.
2. Mix the soured cream with the beaten egg.
3. In a separate bowl, mix flour, sugar, baking powder, bicarbonate of soda and salt.
4. Add sultanas and mix through.
5. Next add the egg and soured cream mixture and mix lightly until you have a soft dough.
6. Turn out onto a well-floured worktop and roll out lightly to about 1.75 inches / 4 cm high.
7. Cut out into scone shapes, 5 for large scones, or aboudt 10 for smaller scones.
8. Transfer gently to prepared baking tin and put in oven. After 10 minutes reduce oven temperature to 180C / 350F / Gas Mark 4, and bake for a further 10 to 15 minutes.

Dairy-Free Fadge Soda Bread

Ingredients:
- 335g / 12 oz / 2.8 cups wholemeal flour
- 110g / 4 oz / 1 cup plain flour
- 2 large or 3 small eggs
- 85g / 3 oz lard
- 85g / 3 oz dripping or lactose-free margarine
- 1 slightly rounded teaspoon bicarbonate of soda
- 1 slightly rounded teaspoon baking powder
- 1/4 teaspoon salt
- 1 dessertspoon vinegar

Method:
1. Put all the dry ingredients into a bowl.
2. Rub in the fats finely.
3. Whisk the eggs well, then whisk the vinegar into the beaten eggs.
4. Add to the dry ingredients to form a stiff dough.
5. Roll out into a circle with a diameter about the length of a new pencil.
6. Cut into 4 triangles.
7. Bake at 375F / 190C / Gas Mark 5 - 400F / 200C / Gas Mark 6 for 15 - 20 minutes.

Serve hot or cold, buttered and spread with jam.

Narrator: The above recipe is one of the more unusual ones for Fadge Bread. There are many differing descriptions of what Fadge Bread actually was. Some say it was a type of soda bread, others that it was a 'wadge' of potato bread, fried. Yet other accounts talk of a very soft, egg-yellow soda bread, full of plump, juicy raisins. Fadge Bread seems to have varied in form according to wherabouts in Ireland it was made. All nostalgic accounts agree however, 'there was nothing quite like Fadge bread'.

Thursday 25th May 1905
Cavan

Dear Eliza,

Thanks for the recipes. We all loved them. I've sent them on to Sophia too. Mam says do you have a good recipe for ground rice pudding? We have tried but think there must be a better recipe around than the way ours turns out!

Mam says to give you our recipe for Buttermilk Oaten Bread. We make this often. You just have to remember to steep the oatmeal in the buttermilk for about 6 hours before baking it. Sometimes we steep it overnight and make the bread the next morning. It's a really simple bread. I love it. Mam says there's something in oats that's good for your mind. If you eat oats regularly they help you from feeling downcast. Father says we should give this recipe to Mrs Lynch down the road. She's always whingeing and moaning about something!

Buttermilk Oaten Bread

Ingredients:
- 310g / 11 oz / 2 cups medium oatmeal
- 470 ml / 2 cups buttermilk or sour milk (+ about ½ cup / 115ml extra to bind)
- 270g / 10 oz / 2.5 cups plain flour
- 1 rounded teaspoon bicarbonate of soda
- ½ level teaspoon salt

Method:
1. Steep oatmeal for about 6 hours, or overnight in the buttermilk.
2. Preheat oven to 400F /200C / Gas Mark 6.
3. Mix flour, salt and bicarbonate of soda together.
4. Stir in the steeped oatmeal.
5. If necessary add a little more buttermilk, but keep the mixture stiff.

6. Put on to a floured worktop and knead lightly until smooth.
7. Roll out into a circle about 5 cm / 2 inches thick.
8. Mark into four, cutting 2/3 way into the bread but do not cut right through. Ease pieces apart just a little.
9. Set on a greased and floured baking tin and put in oven. After 5 minutes reduce oven to 375F /190C / Gas Mark 5.
10. Bake for a total of 25 to 30 minutes.
11. Wrap in a cloth and set on a cooling tray to allow bread to steam out.

I hope you like it Eliza. Sophia still makes it in The States; she says everyone in the house likes it sliced and covered with raspberries. I like it with stewed apple. She has asked Mam to keep sending as many recipes as possible. I know it's hard work and she must feel so lonesome. When I write to her I try to not talk about things that would make her sad for home. The primroses, scarlet pimpernel and all the pretty bluebells on the little path by the river where we used to walk and play just remind me of Sophia so much. I miss her so badly Eliza.
Looking forward to hearing from you soon,

With love,
Lillie

Narrator: Though oats have been recognised as a superfood in Ireland for centuries, more recent studies have highlighted the health benefits they can provide. The October 2014 supplement issue of the British Journal of Nutrition, entitled 'Oats, More Than Just a Whole Grain' confirms that oats have many potential benefits for human health. The Irish have always known too, that if you feed your horses plenty of oats, it will make them rather wild and energetic! Oats are also recognised as having properties which are soothing to the brain and nervous system, and Irish Buttermilk Oaten Bread is a great way to enjoy oats for those who aren't so fond of porridge.

Friday 30th June 1905
Belfast

Dear Lillie,

Thank you for the buttermilk oaten bread recipe. Even Granny said it was good. She does pride herself on her secret recipes and loves to think that no one could ever make anything quite as special as she can. She's a wizard with puddings too. Here's her ground rice pudding recipe –

Border of Rice with Plums

Ingredients:
- 110g / 4 oz / 0.7 cups ground rice
- 1135 ml / 4.8 cups milk
- 55g / 2 oz / 1/2 stick fresh butter
- 55g / 2 oz / 1/4 cup caster sugar
- 2 egg yolks
- 1 bayleaf or vanilla essence

Method:
1. Grease a border pudding mould well with butter and set aside. If you don't have a border mould use a regular one and set an oiled jam jar half filled with water in the centre to create a hollow.
2. Moisten the ground rice with some of the cold milk, boil the remainder with the bayleaf or vanilla essence, then pour it over the rice.
3. Return all to the saucepan. Add the butter and boil all until thick. As the mixture is thickening add the sugar and egg yolks, stirring well.
4. Remove the bayleaf.
5. Pour into the buttered border mould; when cold, turn out on a glass dish and fill the centre with a compote of plums.

Granny baked her special fruit soda bread today and I watched her like a hawk to find out why her fruit soda is so different to anyone else's. It is so rich you don't even need jam on it. Here's how she does it:

Granny's Extra Special Fruit Soda Bread

Ingredients:
- 335g / 12 oz / 3 cups plain flour
- 110g / 4 oz / 1 stick butter or soft margarine
- 85g / 3 oz / 3/8 cup caster sugar
- 110g / 1/4 lb mixed dried fruit
- 1/2 teaspoon ground ginger
- 1/2 teaspoon ground cinnamon
- 1 rounded teaspoon bicarbonate of soda
- 284 ml / 1/2 imperial pint / 1.2 cups buttermilk

Method:
1. Preheat the oven to 190C / 375F / Gas Mark 5. Grease and flour a round cake tin 7 inch / 17.5 cm in diameter, 3 inch / 7.5 cm deep.
2. Rub the butter or soft margarine into the flour.
3. Add the sugar, fruit and spices and mix well.
4. Stir the bicarbonate of soda into the buttermilk to dissolve. Mix this into the dry ingredients.
5. Spoon into tin and gently smooth evenly across top.
6. Bake for 45 minutes, or until well cooked through. Remove from oven, wrap in a clean tea towel and set on a wire tray to cool.

Granny is so proud of her special fruit soda bread that she has never even showed Mother how to make it. Wouldn't it be funny if you were to send this recipe to Sophia, and people all over the States started making my Granny's secret fruit soda bread recipe?

Love,
Eliza

Narrator: Many Irish great-grandmothers and grandmothers were disinclined to pass on their culinary secrets to their daughters and grand-daughters. Some carried the secret of great breads and cakes to their graves rather than give away the power and prestige that being the best wheaten bread or fruit cake maker gave them. Many a daughter was made to think they weren't just as clever as their mother simply because the mother would conceal some little part of the recipe when showing the daughter how to make it. In this way she would ensure that no-one could outshine her as a baker.

It may seem selfish and mean-spirited, but is a little easier to understand when one considers the low status that ordinary married women were given in this often small-minded, repressive society. Of the authentic Irish recipes which have survived, there is frequently another challenge too. Recipes demanded a certain degree of mind-reading on the part of the reader, with much of the method and baking instructions frequently omitted. Many recipes in Queens College Cookbook published in 1907 listed ingredients only, perhaps in the assumption that any accomplished baker could work the method out for themselves.

Sometimes too, family recipes were written down for the author's eyes only, leaving out the parts of the recipe which they knew off by heart.

The following recipe is printed exactly as it appeared in Elizabeth Carmichael-Ferrall's 1913 'Augher Cookbook'.

Toffee (OLD RECEIPT)

Some treacle, some ginger, some sugar, some butter, some lemons, some spice. Boil.

MRS. STOKES, 16 Howell, Exeter.

Friday August 25th 1905
Cavan

Dear Eliza,
        Thank you for your grandma's recipes. They are so good. We've sent them over to Sophia in Brooklyn. She's getting along great and is learning so much over there. She has made friends with a girl called Bridget, who comes from Cork. Bridget gave Sophia her Mam's recipe which she uses if she has ran out of buttermilk, or if she just has too much milk in the house needing to be used up. I like it with soups or sea food. Isn't it great how many different recipes there are for Irish brown bread? Each one is so different - even different people can manage to make the same recipe unique to themselves. I think it's to do with how light a touch one has, or how well you know your own oven, and learning the exact moment when bread is baked just right. I would never have thought that you could make such great Irish brown bread without using buttermilk though.
It's good that Sophia has made a new friend from home. Sophia seems very proud of all the friends she's making out in The States. She's reading a lot too - Mrs Logan said she's welcome to make use of the books in the family library. Sophia says she would never get the quarter of them read in a lifetime, but she does love looking through all the inspirational ones that have maxims and proverbs to live by. She has started to keep a little brown book with all her favourite ones which she comes across. She sent me some in her last letter. If she were to come home now I think she'd be a very different person than she was before she left. Do you think we would change much if we were to go away Eliza? Here is Bridget's recipe and the sayings which Sophia sent me too.

I look forward to your letters so much. Please write soon,
                                        Love,
                                        Lillie

Bridget's Fresh Milk Wheaten Bread Recipe

Ingredients:
(Careful, the wholemeal flour is used half in each bowl)
- 1.5 pints / 728mls / just a little over 3 cups milk
- 900g / 2 lb / 7.5 cups wholemeal flour
- 225g / 8 oz / 1.9 cups plain flour
- 2 level teaspoons salt
- 15 level teaspoons baking powder, sieved (yes, it seems a lot, but this large wheaten needs it)
- 65g / 2.5 oz / 1/4 cup white baking fat
- 1 tablespoon treacle
- 1 egg
- milk and small handful of wholemeal flour to sprinkle over top

Method:
1. In a large bowl put the following:
- All the milk
- Half the wholemeal flour
- All the plain flour

Mix all together and leave to steep for 1 hour

2. In a separate large bowl put the following:
- The other half of the wholemeal flour
- The salt and baking powder
- Rub in the white baking fat very finely.

3. After the one hour steeping time is up, preheat oven to 220 C / 425 F / Gas Mark 7. Mix treacle and beaten egg into the milky mixture and stir lightly.
4. Add the dry bowl ingredients and mix until combined. Do not over mix.
5. Turn out onto a well-floured worktop, quickly shape into a soft oval dough, and transfer to greased and floured roasting tin. Mark into 4 and leave to stand for 10 minutes.
6. Glaze with a little milk, dust a little wholemeal flour across the top of the bread and set into oven. After 10 minutes reduce heat to 200 C / 400 F / Gas Mark 6. Bake for a total of approximately 35 – 45 minutes.
7. Remove from oven, wrap in a clean tea towel and cool on a wire tray.

Sophia's Maxims, Quotes & Sayings

(Sophia says these ones are all old Irish sayings, and is surprised how much Irish writing she's coming across in the States)

'Don't postpone your betterment'

'The richest dish is no better than the ready dish that serves one's pupose'

'Don't make little of your dish, for it may be an ignorant person who judges it'

'However long you remain away from home, don't bring back a bad story about yourself' (Sophia says this is a favourite saying among the Irish in America)

'The night and the day are as long as they ever were' (Our chances are just as good as those of any who went before us)

Old Irish Triad
'Three things that bring misfortune -
drink, jealousy and contention.
Three things that bring prosperity-
Thriftiness, mending and early rising.'

'If you see a pig's head on the cow, don't tell it'

'The person of the greatest talk is the person of the least work'

'Little talk is easy to cure'

Saturday 2nd September 1905
Belfast

Dear Lillie,
That wheaten bread recipe is great - we always thought wheaten bread had to be made with buttermilk to work.
Mother loved Sophia's sayings; they reminded her of a writer Mr Chapman liked in the States. She said some of his words meant so much to her when she was out there that she'll never forget them. His name was John Boyle O'Reilly, an Irishman who was much loved in the States. I have written them out along with my recipe for rhubarb crumble.
I'm glad Sophia is making so many friends. Mother says it's true that going away changes one. But she also says it's good for the character. She has such great memories of her years in America.

                        Love,
                        Eliza

'Rules of The Road'

'Every man on the planet has just as much right as yourself to the road'

'Trust toil, not intent, or your plans will miscarry'

'You're worth what you saved, not the million you made'

'Take gifts with a sigh, most men give to be paid'

Rhubarb Crumble

Ingredients:
- 500g / 1 lb 2 oz rhubarb
- 170g / 6 oz / 3/4 cup granulated or caster sugar

Crumble
- 170g / 6 oz /1.5 cups plain flour
- 85g / 3 oz / 3/4 stick butter
- 55g /2 oz / 1/4 cup granulated or caster sugar

Method:
1. Preheat oven to 375 F / 190 C / gas mark 5, and prepare rhubarb, discarding leaves. Cut into small pieces and put in base of ovenproof dish.
2. Sprinkle with 170g / 6 oz / 3/4 cup sugar.
3. Make crumble topping - Rub butter into flour until it looks like fine breadcrumbs.
4. Add 55g /2 oz / 1/4 cup sugar and sprinkle over fruit in bowl.
5. Put in oven and cook for 15 minutes. Turn heat down to 325 F / 170 C / gas mark 3 and bake for another 45 minutes or so until golden and rhubarb is well cooked. Serve with custard or whipped cream.

Narrator: John Boyle O'Reilly (1844 - 1890) was an Irish Republican who was sentenced to death for recruiting 80 men in his British army regiment to the Irish Republican Brotherhood. The sentence was reduced to 20 years penal servitude in Australia, from where he escaped after several years, eventually ending up in America. He settled in Boston where he began working as a reporter for The Boston Pilot. His frank reports and ability to criticise his fellow countrymen when critisism was due gained him credit as a writer. He went on to establish himself as a well-known humanitarian, writer, poet and orator despite his militant roots, developing a wiseness and tolerance for which he is still remembered today. One of John F. Kennedy's favourite poets, the American President quoted Boyle widely in his address before the Irish Parliament on 28 June 1963 in Dublin, just under 5 months before his assassination on 22 November 1963.

Monday 2nd October 1905
Cavan

Dear Eliza,

    I really am enjoying harvest time this year! Michael and I have been helping out at Paddy's farm for the last few weeks. The best part is sitting down in the grass for a rest with a big tin mug of hot tea and plates full of freshly made soda bread. Paddy's Mam's bread is always still warm and her home churned butter melts right into it. She makes all types of jam; her rhubarb and ginger, apple jelly and blackberry jam all taste so lovely. I asked her for some jam recipes and she gave me my favourite one. Mam sometimes sends an apple tart and her teabread with us to share whenever we go to the farm.

Teabread's probably one of the easiest things you ever could make. Some people soak the fruit in stout but Mam always uses Earl Grey Tea. The oil of Bergamot in the brew makes Mam's teabread taste that little bit nicer than any others I've tried.

Mam's Irish Teabread

Ingredients:
- 175g / 6.5 oz / 1 cup mixed dried fruit
- 160 mls / 2/3 cup strained black Earl Grey Tea
- 2 small to medium sized eggs, beaten
- 110g / 4 oz / 0.7 cups light brown sugar
- 135g / 5 oz / 1.25 cups self-raising flour
- 1/4 teaspoon mixed spice

Method:
1. If mixed fruit contains peel, cut the peel up finely. Soak fruit in the tea for a few hours, or overnight.
2. Preheat the oven to 325F / 170 C / Gas mark 3. Grease and line a 900g / 2 lb / 23 x 13 x 7cm loaf tin.

3. Stir the beaten eggs into the fruit mixture, then add the sugar, flour and spice, and mix well.
4. Put the mixture into the lined tin and spread evenly. Bake for 45 – 60 minutes until cooked through.

Summer Fruits Jam

Ingredients:
- 2 lb gooseberries
- 1.5 lb raspberries
- 1.5 lb redcurrants
- approximately 5 lb sugar

Method:
1. Wash the fruit, take the stalks off the redcurrants and top and tail the gooseberries.
2. Weigh the fruit, and to each 1 lb of fruit use 1 lb of sugar.
3. Put the fruit and sugar in a preserving pan and heat gently until the sugar has melted, then stir constantly until it comes to the boil.
4. Boil for about an hour, until a little tested on a plate has reached setting point.
5. Pot in the usual way.

Frank and Father are working really hard on the roads at the minute. It's time Cavan got some new roads and Father is glad of the extra money. I love when they are so busy because it means I will be able to get some of the latest books for Christmas. Here is my list of new books I would like:
"*The Lady Cake-Maker*" by L.T. Meade
"*By Beach and Bog Land*" by Jane Barlow
"*Ideas of Good and Evil*" by W.B. Yeats
"*The Garden of the Bees & other Poems*" by Seosamh Mac Cathmhaoil (he wrote the words of the air "*My Lagan Love*")
Even if I get two of the books I'll be happy! What books do you like to read Eliza?
Please write back soon,
      Lillie

Tuesday 2nd January 1906
Belfast

Dear Lillie,

A very Happy New Year to you all! We had a lovely Christmas. I got a little box filled with money, which I shall save for some day when I really need it. Did you get the books you wanted? I never ask for books as Granny lets me read all hers. My favourite ones are by William Butler Yeats. Granny's most recent one of his is called *"The Celtic Twilight"*. He's right when he says "It is one of the great troubles of life that we cannot have any unmixed emotions. There is always something in our enemy that we like, and something in our sweetheart that we dislike. It is this entanglement of moods which makes us old, and puckers our brows and deepens the furrows about our eyes. If we could love and hate with as good heart as the faeries do, we might grow to be long-lived like them."

Now Christmas is over we're back to everyday food again here. It does taste great after all the richness of Christmas cooking.

Mother's Stuffed Sausages

Ingredients:
- 6 Irish pork sausages
- 6 slices of bacon
- 6 heaped tablespoons breadcrumbs
- 1 onion, chopped finely and sautéed in a little butter
- 1 dessertspoon finely chopped parsley

Method:
1. Preheat oven to 190C / 375F / Gas Mark 5
2. Mix sautéed onion with parsley and breadcrumbs.
3. Make a cut nearly the length of each sausage, leaving a little bit uncut at each end.
4. Open them out a little and fill the cavity with stuffing.
5. Stretch the bacon and wrap a slice round each stuffed sausage.

6. Bake for 25 – 35 minutes until cooked through.

When Mother was in The States she learnt how to make this apple pudding recipe from Mr Chapman's cook.

Apple Sponge Pudding
Ingredients:
Base
- 1 tablespoon butter
- 55g / 2 oz / 1/4 cup brown sugar
- 4 apples

Sponge Cake Dough
- 110g / 4 oz / 1/2 cup caster sugar
- 2 eggs, separated
- 1.5 tablespoons cold water
- 55g / 2 oz / 1/2 cup plain flour, sieved and mixed with 1/2 teaspoon baking powder
- 1/2 teaspoon vanilla essence
- a handful of flaked almonds

Method:
1. Butter an ovenproof pudding dish. Sprinkle base with the brown sugar.
2. Peel and slice the apples and put in layers in the bottom of the pudding dish.
3. Bake until partially soft. Remove from oven and cover with the following sponge:
4. Cream egg yolks and sugar, add beaten egg whites and remaining ingredients.
5. Bake for about 30 minutes at 350F / 180C / Gas Mark 4. Serve hot with custard sauce.

I hope you like these recipes Lillie. Please write soon. I hope everything is going well for Sophia too.

With love,
Eliza

Saturday 5th May 1906
Cavan

Dear Eliza,
      Sorry I've taken so long to write back.
I'm so glad that you like William Butler Yeats too. You're so lucky that your Grandma collects his books. He's right that we don't really appreciate our own country enough, and that local writers should write more about their homeland. I wonder though, will Sophia always look on here as her home, if she settles in The States for good?
I thought of Sophia when I read this,

"I would have our writers and craftsmen of many kinds master this history and these legends, and fix upon their memory the appearance of mountains and rivers and make it all visible again in their arts, so that Irishmen, even though they had gone thousands of miles away, would still be in their own country".

When I talk to Mam about the States she always says "be careful what you wish for"… I know Mam is missing Sophia so much. She has posted her our apple tart recipe. The pastry is quite thick in this. That is how we have always made it in Cavan. I do love it. What way do you make apple tart?

Mam's Irish Apple Tart Recipe (Thick Pastry)

Ingredients:
Pastry:
- 335g /12 oz / 3 cups plain all-purpose flour
- 55g / 2 oz / 1/4 cup caster sugar
- ½ rounded teaspoon bicarbonate of soda
- pinch of salt
- 85g / 3 oz / 3/4 stick butter
- 5 fl oz / 142 ml / 0.6 cups buttermilk
- 1 large egg

Filling:
- 675g / 1.5 lb Irish Bramley cooking apples (weight before peeling)
- 110g -170g / 4-6 oz / 1/2 - 3/4 cup caster sugar

Bake as a round pie or use a deep Swiss roll tin to make into apple squares. If using ordinary sweet apples cut the sugar amount given for the filling.

Method:
1. Sieve the flour, salt, bicarbonate of soda and sugar into a bowl.
2. Chop the butter into small pieces and rub into the flour mixture until all resembles fine breadcrumbs.
3. Whisk the egg, mix with the buttermilk, and add this to the rest of the ingredients in the bowl.
4. Mix to a soft dough and turn out onto a well-floured worktop.
5. Divide mixture in two, and roll out first piece into a round or rectangle, depending on shape of dish or tray used. Grease dish or tin and line with pastry.
6. Preheat the oven to 180C / 350F /Gas Mark 4.
7. Peel the apples and slice them over the pastry base, adding as much sugar as necessary to sweeten them.
8. Roll out the second piece of pastry to form a lid. Seal the edges and prick all over with a fork to allow steam to escape.
9. Sprinkle a little sugar over the top of the pie. Put a lined tray on the shelf below pie to catch any syrup which may bubble out during baking.
10. Bake in the oven for 30 – 45 minutes.
11. If baked in a rectangular or square tin, cut into squares or fingers while still hot. Sprinkle a little more sugar over the top if you wish.

This tastes lovely still warm with custard or whipped cream on top of it. I love the pastry. Buttermilk gives the pastry a really special flavour and smell. Have you seen Tommy since? Paddy is getting on my nerves here. Since Sophia went away he is always turning up pestering me. Sophia is lucky to escape him. He never shuts up. He goes on and on to Frank and Michael too. He always talks as if he is really thinking of something else at the same time.
Mam says the Dublin writer Katharine Tynan spotted this trick around her when she wrote, "and if you win a flow of talk here be sure they are talking

round what they have to tell you by leading you away from it; for an Irishman uses language to conceal his thoughts". I have noticed some people doing it to others, but Katharine Tynan puts thoughts we all have a notion of into words so well Mam says. She really is an honest writer, yet dearly loves her homeland too. She says "When the Irish go away they are lonely for the mountains". I wonder does Sophia miss the mountains. Every time I look at Cuilcagh Mountain I have an aching inside. It's so very beautiful, especially when it's misty, or the clouds are sitting low on Cuilcagh, I get a tingling just staring at it. I think I miss my sister with an even heavier heart when I look at the mountain.

I look forward to your letters and recipes so much Eliza. Please write soon,

Love,
   Lillie

Narrator: Katharine Tynan (1859 -1931) was a close friend of William Butler Yeats. She first met Yeats in June 1885 at her father's thatched farmhouse just outside Dublin. She was 26, Yeats was 20. She had just published her first work 'Louise de la Vallière and other Poems'. Yeats had only just made his debut in the Dublin University Review. They became close friends, corresponding frequently. After about 5 years, Yeats proposed marriage, but Katharine refused, though they still remained good friends.
Katharine married the writer and barrister Henry Hinkson in 1898. They had 3 children; their daughter Pamela Hinkson (1900 - 1982), was also well known for her novels. 'The Ladies' Road,' published in 1932, sold over 100,000 copies in the Penguin edition. In addition to her adult fiction and her girls' school stories, Pamela Hinkson also published novels under the pseudonym 'Peter Deane.'

In 1909 Katharine Hinkson published 'The Book of Flowers' with Frances Maitland. Divided into Spring, Summer, Autumn and Winter, the author was guided to the following rare old 'recipes' pages in her family copy by a single little pressed dried leaf tucked into pages 210 -211 and one at pages 212 -213.

NB: 1 oz = 28 g
Dram measurements varied, but it was at most a small level teaspoon or 3.5 g, in the US apothecaries system it was 1.75g, or one-sixteenth of an ounce.

Pot Pourri

"Gather the roses after the morning dew is off, but before twelve o'clock - they should be well opened (but not full blown the day before they are pulled). Pull off the leaves and spread them in a cloth in the air, but not in the sun, for an hour or two, to take off any remaining moisture, but not long enough to wither them.
Have 1 lb Bay salt (pounded) and 1/2 lb common salt mixed, 1 oz of cloves, 1 oz cinnamon and 2 oz allspice, pounded and mixed. Gather the rose leaves clean off the cloth, discarding any spoilt ones or husks, and put a layer in the bottom of the jar, then lay a layer of salt and spices over them. Fill the jar in this way in layers, and when full turn them up from the bottom and mix them well several times. Cover the top of the jar with a cloth, and let it stand in the sun for some time, for this seems to strengthen the flavour.
Roses are better not mixed, the true Scarlet or the large Cabbage Rose are the best kinds for this. Lavender flowers stripped from the stalk and mixed with the rose leaves is an improvement, this may be added at any time. Leaves of Verbena may also be put in when to be had."

Sweet-Scented Bags to Lay With Linen

"8 oz coriander seeds, 8 oz sweet orrice-root, 8 oz damask rose leaves, 8 oz calamus aromaticus, 1 oz mace, 1 oz cinnamon, 1/2 oz cloves, 4 drams musk powder, 2 drams white loaf sugar, 3 oz lavender flowers and some Rhodium wood; beat them well together and make them up in small silk bags."

Monday 3rd September 1906
Belfast

Dear Lillie,

We've had such beautiful weather here over the last few days. I really love autumn. I have heard nothing of Tommy, nor nothing of Aunt Annie either. Maybe we shall see her at Christmas. I have been trying to put him to the back of my head, but that doesn't always work!
I love what William Butler Yeats says about art. He says to be bold with our creativity and not care what others think. I think if people go around worried about others approval, they're never going to win at anything. There's always some negative person round the corner ready to put one down! When I listen to Granny and all her poetry I realise how much importance was placed on poems, ballads and dreaming in the old days. Granny says people need to learn how to "get over themselves" and that our poets and dreamers can help us do that.
It's blackberry time again Lillie. I've been watching them ripen all last week. Every autumn since I was little I've picked blackberries. Here's one of the desserts I make with them. I hope you get time to make it before the blackberries are all gone.

Orange & Blackberry Pudding

Ingredients:
- 310g / 11 oz blackberries
- 28g / 1 oz / 1/4 stick butter
- 110g / 4 oz / 1/2 cup caster sugar & some extra to sweeten blackberries
- 2 large eggs, at room temperature, separated
- grated rind and all the juice of 1 small to medium sized orange -
- 55g / 2 oz / 1/2 cup self raising flour
- powdered / icing sugar to dust

Method:
1. Wash blackberries well, and line the bottom of an ovenproof dish with them.
2. Dust some sugar over these to sweeten (and form a sauce when cooked) and leave to soak in.
3. In a separate bowl, cream butter with the sugar, add the egg yolks and beat well.
4. Add orange rind and juice and mix through.
5. Add flour and combine well. Beat egg whites until they form stiff peaks.
6. Fold these well into the mixture.
7. Pour all over the blackberries.
8. Set the dish in a tray with about 2.5 cm / 1 inch of water surrounding it.
9. Bake at 180 C / 350 F / Gas Mark 4 for 30 - 40 minutes until risen and golden. Dust with powdered icing sugar to decorate.

I asked Granny had she heard of Katherine Tynan after I read your last letter. Granny really loves her poetry, especially one poem called "The Wind That Shakes the Barley". I wrote it out for you because it is so beautiful. Granny thinks Katharine Tynan is writing here about the Dublin and Wicklow mountains she grew up beside.

Here's our recipe for Autumn Jelly. I should have sent this to you sooner, but you should still get time to make it before the hedges and trees are bare. The cake is great because it's made with blackberry jam so you can make it anytime of the year. Please write soon,

Love,
Eliza

Autumn Jelly

Ingredients:
- 1.5 kg / 3 lb crab or windfall apples
- 1.5 kg / 3 lb blackberries
- 1.5 kg / 3 lb elderberries, sloes, hips and haws
- 450g / 1 lb sugar to every 450 ml / 1 lb liquid

Method:
1. Wash and chop apples and barely cover with water. Simmer until soft and leave to strain through a jelly bag or muslin.
2. Wash blackberries thoroughly, checking for small insects, barely cover with water. Simmer until soft and leave to strain through bag or muslin.
3. Wash remaining berries, pricking sloes and topping and tailing hips and haws. Barely cover with water. Simmer until soft and leave to strain through a jelly bag or muslin.
4. Mix all strained juices together and add 450g / 1 lb sugar to every 450 ml / 1 lb liquid.
5. Simmer gently to dissolve sugar, then boil until setting point is reached.
6. Pot and cover as usual in warm sterilised jars.

Blackberry Cake

Ingredients:
- 110g / 4 oz / 1/2 cup butter
- 225 g / 8 oz / 1 cup caster sugar
- 4 teaspoons cold water
- 1 teaspoon bicarbonate of soda
- 2 eggs, separated
- 225g / 8 oz / 2 cups plain flour
- 280g / 10 oz / 1 cup blackberry jam
- 1 teaspoon cinnamon
- 1/2 teaspoon cloves

Method:
1. Preheat oven to 350F / 180C / Gas Mark 4.
2. Sieve flour and soda together 3 times. Add spices.
3. Cream butter and sugar together until very light.
4. Add beaten yolks, blackberry jam, and water, alternately with flour mixture.
5. Beat egg whites stiff and fold in.
6. Bake in a lined loaf tin for about 45 minutes until baked through.
7. Cool and cover with plain icing.

The Wind That Shakes the Barley

Katharine Tynan

There's music in my heart all day,
I hear it late and early,
It comes from fields are far away,
The wind that shakes the barley.

Above the uplands drenched with dew
The sky hangs soft and pearly,
An emerald world is listening to
The wind that shakes the barley.

Above the bluest mountain crest
The lark is singing rarely,
It rocks the singer into rest,
The wind that shakes the barley.

Oh, still through summers and through springs
It calls me late and early.
Come home, come home, come home, it sings,
The wind that shakes the barley.

Thursday 4th October 1906
Cavan

Dear Eliza,
      We all loved your recipes, and they came just in time. Thank you. Katharine Tynan's poem is really beautiful. I was going to send it to Sophia, but then I changed my mind. I was worried it wouldn't be fair to make someone who's been brave enough to go away, feel homesick. Sophia is becoming such a strong person in the States. She's sent me more of the proverbs she's collecting including one from John Boyle O'Reilly.
She said Mrs Logan dined out recently at the Brighton Beach Hotel in Brooklyn. She had a meal of Kennebec salmon, asparagus and German fried potatoes, followed by Nesselrode pudding. Sophia says Nesselrode pudding is a type of ice dessert with fruit which has been poached in syrup to stop it freezing hard in the ice cream. It's flavoured with maraschino liqueur. Doesn't it sound lovely? The family Sophia works for are very wealthy.
 Here's 2 little breakfast recipes; they're simple but a fry wouldn't be the same without them! I hope you like them. Please write soon,
                                            Love,
                                            Lillie

Irish Potato Bread

Ingredients:
- 225g / 8 oz / 1 cup warm boiled potato
- 2 x 15 ml tablespoons melted butter
- 28 -55g / 1-2 oz / 1/4 - 1/2 cup plain flour
- Approx. 55g / 2 oz / 1/3 cup cooked bacon, cut up as small as possible

Method:
1. Mash potato, season with salt and pepper, and put through a potato ricer to remove any lumps.

2. Place riced potatoes and bacon in a bowl, add butter, and sift in enough flour to bind to a dough.
3. Knead lightly on a worktop dusted with flour. Roll out to about 0.6 cm / 1/4 of an inch.
4. Place a plate on top and cut around the circle. Mark into quarter pieces.
5. Dry fry very slowly on a low heat in a heavy based pan or a griddle – There's no need for any oil as the butter in the dough is enough.

Fried Tomatoes

Cut tomatoes in half and fry inside down at first. Turn and sprinkle some brown sugar into the cooked side, continue to cook the outside base to your liking.

Sophia's Maxims, Quotes & Sayings

'Be silent and safe - silence never betrays you
Be true to your word and your work and your friend
Put least trust in him who is foremost to praise you
Nor judge of a road till it draws to the end'
(John Boyle O'Reilly)

'It's a long road that there's no turn in'

'Many a misty morning developed into a good day'

'To make a beginning is a third of the work'

'You'll never plough a field by turning it over in you mind'

'What would cure one person would kill another person'

'Don't put your hook in a field without being asked' (That is, don't begin to reap your neighbour's corn till he asks you. People sometimes are displeased even by our offering to help them in their work.)

Tuesday 27th November 1906
Belfast

Dear Lillie,

       I wonder what the difference is between German fried potatoes and Irish fried potatoes. That meal Sophia described isn't a whole lot different than what we have here at home. We have wonderful Atlantic salmon, beautiful vegetables and the best potatoes in the world. And we don't even have to go near some fancy hotel for them. We just don't know how to make Nesselrode pudding though. To be honest, I think the Gaelic Steak Mother makes Father on a Saturday night would be a fair match for any dinner in any fancy hotel. I've written out the recipe, and also Father's favourite ginger cake. Father likes ginger put into anything it goes with. He says it's good for his stomach. I hope you like the recipe and wish you all a lovely Christmas,

                                                   Love,
                                                   Eliza

Gaelic Steak

Ingredients for one person:
- 1 fillet steak
- 28g / 1 oz / 1/4 stick butter
- 30 ml / 2 tablespoons cream
- 30 ml / 2 tablespoons Irish whiskey

Method:
1. Fry steak in melted butter.
2. Remove from pan and drain.
3. Add cream and whiskey to pan and combine together.
4. Pour over steak and serve with garden vegetables.

Ginger Sponge Squares

Ingredients:
236 ml / 1 cup milk
4 x 15 ml level tablespoons golden / corn syrup
110g / 4 oz / 1 stick butter
225g / 8 oz / 2 cups self-raising flour
225g / 8 oz / 1 cup sugar
2 heaped teaspoons ground ginger
1 rounded teaspoon bicarbonate of soda
1 egg, whisked

Method:
1. Line a 25cm / 9 inch square tin (depth 5cm / 2 inches) with greaseproof paper. Preheat oven to 170C / 325F / Gas Mark 3.
2. Melt milk, golden / corn syrup and butter together in a saucepan and let cool a little.
3. Weigh out the self-raising flour, sugar, ground ginger, and bicarbonate of soda and sieve them into a bowl.
4. Combine dry ingredients with melted mixture.
5. Add one whisked egg and mix all together.
6. Transfer to prepared tin and bake for about 45 minutes until cooked through.
7. Cut into squares to serve.

Narrator: It would have been difficult for Eliza and Lillie to make Nesselrode pudding without a freezer, but that's not to say that it couldn't be done. A rather complicated recipe for Nesselrode Pudding had appeared in Alexis Soyer's Gastronomic Regenerator published in 1846 just as the Great Famine was breaking out in Ireland. Alexis Soyer was well-known in Ireland as the French chef appointed by Britain to assist in famine relief. He arrived in Dublin in April 1847, setting up soup kitchens to distribute his nourishing 'Famine Soup' of vegetables, barley and beef bones. It was not always well received, with many poor failing to realise the nutritive value of the beef bones and scorning his efforts.

Easter 1907
Cavan

Dear Eliza,

Oh I'm so glad it's springtime again. The new lambs are out running about in the fields now. Father has all his drills of potatoes planted. Mam and I have spring cleaned the whole house. I love Easter.
There's been a huge fire raging over the mountainous land owned by Lord Rossmore for the last five days. Father says it covered 300 acres and has only just stopped burning.
I've baked Grandma's old Irish cheesecake recipe and it's sitting in the pantry ready for tomorrow. It tastes perfect when it's just getting cold, but not really cold. Here is the recipe.

Old Irish Buttermilk Cheesecake

Pastry:
- 225g / 8 oz / 2 cups plain flour
- 110g / 4 oz / 1 stick butter
- 1 egg
- 50g / 2 oz/ 1/4 cup caster sugar

Topping:
- ¾ imperial pint / 425 ml / 1.8 cups buttermilk
- 3 large eggs
- 3 rounded 15ml tablespoons plain flour, sieved
- 225g / 8 oz / 1 cup caster sugar
- 110 g / 4 oz / 1 stick slightly melted butter
- a pinch of salt
- 2 teaspoons vanilla essence

(Use a round spring form cake tin 23cm / 9 inch in diameter)

Method:
To make pastry shell:
1. Lightly rub butter into flour.
2. In a small bowl, combine egg and caster sugar to make a paste. Add this to the flour mixture and bind together to form pastry.
3. Roll out on a well-floured worktop, dusting with more flour as needed.
4. Lightly grease and line spring form tin with the pastry, taking pastry at least 5cm / 2 inches up the sides of tin.
5. Preheat oven to 425 F / 220 C / Gas Mark 7.

To make cheesecake topping:
1. Sieve flour, sugar and salt into a large bowl.
2. Separate eggs and set aside whites. Beat egg yolks a little and mix with the buttermilk, vanilla and lightly melted butter.
3. Add these to the flour mixture and lightly mix together until combined.
4. Beat egg whites until they form stiff peaks. Fold these into the rest of the batter.
5. Pour into pastry shell and place in preheated oven. Reduce oven heat immediately to 325 F / 170 C / Gas Mark 3. Bake for approximately 50 minutes, until set.

Grandma's recipe is really old but I do love it. She says it's one of the most ancient recipes in Ireland. She can even remember her grandmother making it. I hope you're having a lovely Easter. Please write soon.

Love,
Lillie

Tuesday June 4th, 1907
Belfast

Dear Lillie,

You're never going to believe this. Mother took me to Queen's College fundraising fête and I bought an amazing cookery book at the Mayflower stall there. The rain just poured down all day – there was about an inch of it! There was even thunder and lightning! I felt so sorry for all the ladies who had put so much effort into the fête.

Lots of local people sent in their best recipes to publish in a book to raise money for a new athletics field for Queen's College here in Belfast. Lady Londonderry helped them with it (she's a senator of Queen's College). There's even a recipe from Lady Whitla, who is a friend of Florence Nightingale's.

We saw Lady Londonderry there too. She has really got a special way with her and is very popular. Her friends just call her Nellie! It's no wonder she managed to get so many people to part with their recipes for the book. She's just one of those people who draws others to her.

Guess what Lillie… Mother says back in the eighties Lady Londonderry's husband discovered she was having an affair with Harry Cust. Harry Cust was the MP for Bermondsey up until last year and was also the editor of the Pall Mall Gazette. Some people call him Henry. Apparently Lord Londonderry found out when Lady de Grey, who was also having an affair with Harry, posted Nellie's love letters to Harry back to Nellie's husband. He must have been very upset, but it seems that they are getting on okay again now.

Did you know that their daughter-in-law Edith has a winding snake tattoo that runs right up her leg, starting at her ankle? Apparently she had it done four years ago when she was on a second honeymoon with her husband in Japan. They are definitely one of the most unconventional families Belfast has ever seen. Mother says the nice thing about them is that even though they they're very wealthy they have a lot of empathy for others.

Granny speaks highly of them too. She says that back in the time of the Great Famine here Lady Londonderry's husband's great-aunt, Frances Anne Vane, Marchioness of Londonderry provided much needed employment in the

Glens. In the first years of the famine she started the building and laying out of the grounds of Garron Tower. This gave work to many local people and tided them over those years of hunger. A man called Francis Turnley put gangs of men to work building roads in the area too. Grandmother says their commonsense attitude saved many lives. It's terrible to think that over a million people died in Ireland such a short time ago. Frances Anne Vane's great grandson is that young up and coming politician Winston Churchill. Winston's mother is an American called Jennie Jerome who grew up in Brooklyn, New York!

I've just started looking through the new cookery book and Mary Maxton has put in a recipe for scrambled eggs and tomatoes. Her husband James Maxton is a Naval Architect and works in the shipbuilding industry here. I wonder does he know Tommy... Aunt Annie says Tommy loves simple food the best- it looks like Mary's husband does too!

Tomato and Egg Scramble
By Mary Edwards Maxton

1. Peel 4 large vine tomatoes (by dipping in scalding water), slice, and stew them in a little country butter for 15 minutes.
2. Beat 2 best quality eggs, add them to the tomatoes, and scramble them until the eggs are cooked. Serve on buttered toast.

It really does feel as cold as winter here at the moment. I wish the sun would come out again. Aunt Annie told Mother that Tommy brings sunshine into the house when he walks in from work each evening. Can you imagine her saying that? He returned from Comber last weekend with a pot of some of his own honey to share. He told Aunt Annie that he has nine hives of bees on the land at his parent's home. She says Tommy's favourite book at the moment is "*The Life of the Bee*" by Maurice Maeterlinck. He told her it's one of the most profound books ever written. Granny's old Oaten Honeycomb recipe would be perfect for him. Granny says people have been making it here for as long as she can remember.

Oaten Honeycomb

Ingredients:
- 568 ml /1 imperial pint of milk
- 110 g/ 4 oz / one heaped cup porridge oats
- 28g / 1 oz / 1/8 cup butter
- 55 g / 2 oz / 1/2 cup ground almonds or hazelnuts
- 55 g / 2 oz/ 1/4 cup caster sugar
- 1/2 level teaspoon ground cinnamon
- finely grated zest of one orange
- 4 x 15 ml tablespoons honey
- 3 eggs, separated
- extra honey to drizzle over top

Method:
1. Bring milk to the boil, add oats, and cook gently for a few minutes.
2. Add butter, stirring well until it has melted in. Let the mixture cool.
3. Mix in the ground almonds, honey, sugar, and orange zest and egg yolks.
4. Beat egg whites stiffly until they form peaks, and fold in.
5. Transfer to a greased 1.2 litre / 2 pint pudding bowl and cover with a piece of greaseproof paper folded with a pleat to allow space for the pudding to rise. Tie string around the paper to hold it in place.
6. Place the pudding in a steamer or a large saucepan and fill halfway up the sides of the basin with boiling water. Cover and simmer for 2 hours.
7. Serve with plenty of honey drizzled over the top.

Raspberry Jam
by Mrs Mary Champbell

Allow one and a quarter pounds / 560g / 2.5 cups of preserving sugar to each 450g /1 lb of fruit.

Put the sugar in the oven until it becomes very but not scorched.

Bruise the fruit very well, put it in the preserving pan and bring almost to a boiling point.

Take it off the heat and pour in the hot sugar, then stir well until all the sugar is dissolved, then pour into sterilised pots.

Soubise Soup
By Mrs R. McMullan

Ingredients:
- 2 large Spanish onions
- ½ head celery
- 3 pints / 1700ml boiling water
- ½ pint / 284 ml thin cream
- 25g / 1 oz / 1/4 stick of butter
- seasoning
- some freshly grated nutmeg
- 4 x 15ml tablespoons tapioca
- cornflour / corn starch if necessary to thicken (and a little milk to dissolve it in)

Method:
1. Slice onion and celery and fry without browning in butter.
2. Pour over boiling water; add tapioca, seasoning, nutmeg, and boil one hour. Rub through a sieve or liquidise; add cream, and some cornflour / corn starch dissolved in a little milk (if necessary to thicken soup).
3. Serve with croutons.

The last two recipes are from my new Queen's College cookbook. I'll be able to send you lots of recipes now Lillie. It's going to be so much making them all,
   Love,
    Eliza

Tuesday July 2nd 1907
Cavan

Dear Eliza,
        I thought Mary Maxton's tomato and egg scramble was rather nice, but isn't it a bit plain? It made me realise that we're just as good cooks as the next person, and we should have a lot more faith in ourselves than we do. I think Sophia has learnt a lot more self-confidence in America already too Eliza.
That is funny to hear about Lady Londonderry's daughter-in-law's tattoo. Mam said she's heard about Harry Cust. Auntie Ethel knows some of his poetry. She says, 'that sentimental dandy Cust has a great way with words!' I'm sending it to you with this letter Eliza; I wish I could see your face as you read it. It's not the kind of thing the lads round here would write! I can just imagine Paddy sitting down to compose poetry like Harry Cust does.
Sophia is getting on great in America. I can tell from her letters that she has settled in well. I'm beginning to think she actually prefers life there, but doesn't want to hurt us by saying it outright. She's even gone and sent Mam a recipe for creamed potatoes. Does she think we don't know how to cook potatoes here? See what you think of it and let me know,
                                                      Love,
                                                      Lillie

Creamed Potatoes

Ingredients:
- 4 cold boiled potatoes
- 120 ml / 1/2 cup milk
- salt and pepper
- 1/2 teaspoon salt
- 2 tablespoons butter
- 1 tablespoon chopped parsley

Method:
1. Cut the potatoes into cubes or thin slices.
2. Put, with the milk, into a pan or double - boiler and cook until they have absorbed nearly all the milk.
3. Add the butter, seasoning and finely chopped parsley.
4. Cook for 5 more minutes and serve hot.

Narrator:
Henry / Harry Cust (1861 -1917) was a London born politician and jounalist who claimed descent from King Edward III. He went to Eton College in 1874 and Trinity College Cambridge in 1881. He became Conservative MP for Stamford, Lincolnshire in 1890. He was a devastatingly handsome socialite who had numerous affairs. His affair with Violet Manners (1856 - 1937), wife of Lord Granby, produced a daughter, Lady Diana Cooper. This lineage was not acknowledged until well into the twentieth century. Lady Diana Cooper was a close friend of the Queen Mother. In an interview with the Royal biographer Michael Thornton when Cooper was 86, she stated that Beatrice Stephenson, mother of the former British Prime Minister Margaret Thatcher , was also the child of an illicit relationship with Henry Cust. (Thornton, 2013).

EPITAPH ON A DOG

By Henry John Cockayne Cust (sometimes known as Harry)

Here lies
that head and heart of dearness
POPSY BOO
in splendid faithful following of his master's example
the joy of life, the heart of love
worshipped by master, mistress and children
died in a mist of tears
1901
"Who travels now through all that shadowy way"
"from which no sparrows come again, they say"
Ever faithful and following
He loved much and sinned much
But every sin and love he decorated.
bland, suave and prudent
he was blind to a multitude of things he saw and
deaf to a larger multitude of things he heard
and
by his fortunate faculty
of barking at the right moment
he not infrequently saved
the fortunes of the family,
who consecrate
this tribute
of affection to his memory.

Monday August 5th 1907
Belfast

Dear Lillie,
      Thank you for your letter and for writing out that poem by Lady Londonderry's lover. I think it's very sweet. It must be how he wins over all those ladies. Some men around here could do with taking a leaf out of his book! I wonder what he looks like.
Seriously though, I am in trouble. I live for every little tidbit of news about Tommy when Auntie Annie calls to visit. If Auntie Annie wasn't so much older than him I would swear she has fallen for him herself. He sits talking to her at supper and tells her so many things about himself.
The other day he told her a really nice story about some mischief he got up to with his pals. I think it shows what a good, kind person he really is. His heart is always in the right place Aunt Annie says.
When he was still a schoolboy he went on a walking tour during the Easter holidays over the Ards peninsula with some of his school pals. Crossing Strangford Lough at Portaferry, they visited St. John's Point, the most easterly part of Ireland. There, finding the tide in their favour, they crossed the sands from Ballykinler to Dundrum. Tommy carried the youngest of the boys on his back through a deep stretch of water they had to pass through at one point. On they walked to Newcastle and across the mountains to Rostrevor. In their hotel at Rostrevor the boys got a bit carried away while fooling around and broke the rail of a bedstead. Tommy took the blame for this and told the landlady that he would bear the expense of repairing the break. She answered that in her hotel they did not keep patched beds, and so would be troubling him for the cost of a new one. Tommy told her that if that was the case then the old one would belong to him. The landlady said that was fair enough provided he take the old one away! Tommy argued no further, and after talking to a friendly chambermaid, located an old charwoman who said her sick husband would be delighted with the luxury of a bedstead. So Tommy offered to mend it and give it to her. The old lady said to Tommy that it wouldn't be her place to be taking a bed from the hotel. Tommy told her, not to worry about that, asked for her address, and told her to go away and

borrow a screwdriver.

So he and his pals roughly repaired the rail, took the bedstead to pieces, and, applauded by the other guests, carried it to the street. A good-natured tram conductor allowed them to load it on an end of his car. Soon they reached the woman's home, carried in the bedstead, set it up in the little room, raised the old man and his straw mattress upon it from the floor, made him comfortable, and off they went, the old couple showering them with blessings as they went out the door.

He's one in a million Lillie and I can't stop thinking about him every single day.

Anyway, at long last here's Mother's apple tart pastry recipe which you asked for ages ago. I think it's excellent because it stretches so well that you can really roll it out as thinly as you like. I nearly forgot to send it to you, only that we were talking about how everybody has their own way of making it the other day. Sorry it's so long in coming. I think it's dreaming of Tommy that has me all mixed up!

Mother's really thin Apple Tart Pastry

This quantity makes enough for a large 27 cm / 11 inch diameter deep apple tart with some pastry left for a few individual little pies; or you could make 2 medium sized pies, whichever you fancy!

Ingredients:
- 450g / 1 lb / 4 cups plain all-purpose flour
- ½ rounded teaspoon baking powder
- ¼ level teaspoon salt
- 225g / ½ lb lard
- 1 small egg
- 20 ml white vinegar
- 85 ml water
- 12g / ½ oz / 2 heaped teaspoons sugar

Pastry Glaze
- Whipped egg white & caster sugar to sprinkle on top

Method:
1. Put all dry ingredients in a bowl and mix well.
2. Cut fat up into small pieces and rub into flour till it resembles fine breadcrumbs.
3. In a separate bowl blend egg, vinegar and water together.
4. Add this to mixing bowl and bind together. Do not over mix. If very dry add a tiny bit more water. Work quickly with this pastry as it much easier to work with when it is just made.
5. Set out on a well floured worktop and divide in 2. Roll out first piece quite thinly to line base and sides of pie dish.
6. Fill with freshly sliced bramley apples, adding sugar to sweeten.
7. Roll out lid larger than size needed and lay pastry over the top of pie. Gently push down around edge of pie dish to form crust and cut off excess pastry with a knife.
8. Glaze pastry lid of pie with beaten egg white and sprinkle caster sugar on top. Bake at 170C / 325F/ Gas Mark 3 for around an hour, or until well browned.

The apples can leak out a bit, so we always set the pie dishes on top of a large baking tin lined with baking paper before putting them into the oven.

Granny is on one of her poetry reminiscing days again today. It's all about "men's hearts burning and beating", and "stars climbing the dew-dropping sky" here this afternoon. I wonder was Granny's life with Grandpa really as good as she says...
Please write soon Lillie,
    Love,
     Eliza

PS Sophia's recipe for Creamed Potatoes was a bit of a surprise, but I suppose she thought your Mam would be interested in how everything's done a bit differently over there.

Narrator:
Fermanagh born writer John William Bullock, who took the name Shan F. Bullock after Shan Fadh, the title-character in William Carleton's 'Shan Fadh's Wedding;' published the biography 'Thomas Andrews Shipbuilder With an Introduction by Sir Horace Plunkett ' in October 1912. In it he lists the names of the many ships in whose building Andrews had a hand, 'more or less, as Designer, Constructor, Supervisor and Adviser.' The Cedric, the Baltic, the Adriatic, the Oceanic, the Amerika, the President Lincoln and President Grant, the Nieuw Amsterdam, the Rotterdam, the Lapland ,the Olympic and the Titanic.'
'There are many others, less known perhaps, but carrying the flag no less proudly upon the Seven seas, for whose design and construction Andrews was in some measure, often in great measure responsible: the Aragon, the Amazon, the Avon, the Asturias, the Arlanza, the Herefordshire, the Leicestershire, the Gloucestershire, the Oxfordshire, the Pericles, the Themistocles, the Demosthenes, the Laurentic, the Megantic, and the rest. The work of building all those ships, and so many more, from the Celtic to the Titanic, covered a period of some thirteen years, 1899-1912. In 1904 he (Andrews) became Assistant Chief Designer, and in the year following was promoted to be Head of the Designing department under Lord Pirrie. '
He gives insight into how Thomas Andrews went about making his dreams of success come true. 'The long day's work over at the Island, many a young man would have preferred, and naturally perhaps, to spend his evenings pleasurably: not so Tom Andrews. Knowing the necessity, if real success were to be attained, of perfecting himself on the technical as much as on the practical side of his profession, and perhaps having a desire also to make good what he considered wasted opportunities at school, he pursued, during the five years of his apprenticeship, and afterwards too, a rigid course of night studies: in this way gaining an excellent knowledge of Machine and Freehand drawing, of Applied mechanics, and the theory of Naval architecture. So assiduously did he study that seldom was he in bed before eleven o'clock; he read no novels, wasted no time over newspapers; and hardly could be persuaded by his friends to give them his company for an occasional evening.'

Thursday September 12th 1907
Cavan

Dear Eliza,
 Thanks for the apple pie recipe. That really is the thinnest pastry in the world. It is so amazingly fun to roll out!
Oh Eliza, I don't know what to say about going away. Sophia has met so many different types of people already, but still with all she is lonesome for home in her last letter. She says summer has been too hot in New York and she misses Mam's brown bread. She has had to learn to bake things called Parker House Rolls and fancy egg dishes for breakfast. The rest of the cooking is done by Polly, the other domestic servant in the household. Polly gets up at 5 every morning but Sophia doesn't get up until 6, except for Monday which is washday, then she must get up at 5 too. Everyone drinks coffee there, and Sophia has 2 cups every morning by the time everyone has breakfasted in the house.
The thing she hates most is when she gets up to find a lot of dirty dishes from the night before. Mam would never leave dishes out like that. But she just has to be getting on with it Eliza. She says Mr Logan is always asking for curried eggs. I can't imagine Father eating these, and our Michael definitely wouldn't. Sophia sent the recipe in her letter. I thought you'd like a look at it too Eliza.

Curried Eggs

Ingredients:
- 6 hard-boiled eggs
- 28g / 1 oz / 2 tablespoons butter
- 2 x level 15 ml tablespoons flour
- ½ rounded teaspoon curry powder
- 1/8 teaspoon pepper
- 236ml / 1 cup milk
- ¼ teaspoon salt

Method:
1. Melt butter, add flour, seasonings and curry powder, then gradually the milk and simmer until beginning to thicken, whisking gently all the time to avoid lumps.
2. Slice the eggs crosswise, or in eighths lengthwise, and reheat in the sauce.
3. Garnish with bread croutons. One teaspoon of chopped onion may be browned in the butter if desired.

Sophia says these curried eggs taste pretty good, but she keeps wishing she had some of Mam's brown bread with them! Here is Mam's brown bread recipe.

Mam's Brown Soda Bread Recipe

Ingredients:
- 8 oz / 225g / 2 cups medium wholemeal flour
- 2 oz / 55g / 1/2 cup plain white flour
- 2 oz / 55g/ 1/2 stick butter
- 1 level teaspoon bicarbonate of soda
- 1/2 level teaspoon salt
- 1 dessertspoon golden or corn syrup
- 1 dessertspoon dark soft brown sugar
- 250 ml / just over 1 cup buttermilk

Method:
1. Sieve white flour, baking soda, salt and dark brown sugar into a bowl. Add wholemeal flour and mix well.
2. Melt syrup and butter just a little. Make a well in the flours and add melted syrup, butter and buttermilk. Mix all together well.
3. Pour into a well-greased and floured 2 lb loaf tin. Bake at 190 C / 375F / Gas Mark 5 for 40 to 50 minutes until baked through. Remove from tin and wrap in a clean cloth and place on a cooling rack. Remove cloth after 20 minutes and finish cooling.

I love this spread with freshly churned butter and cooked scallops or mussels Eliza. It's lovely too with Irish salmon. Father says that Irish salmon is the sweetest you can eat anywhere in the world. Does your new recipe book have any good recipes for cooking fish in it?

Here's a few more sayings which came with Sophia's last letter too. Strange, she's still sending us Irish quotes!

Do write soon Eliza,

Love,

Lillie

Sophia's Maxims, Quotes & Sayings

'The man who loses the game has leave to shout'
(he should get the satisfaction of giving 'a piece of his mind' explaining how he lost it, or protesting that he did not get fair play)

'The windy day is not the day of the scolbs'
(Thatch is fastened down scolbs or pieces of wood. The negligent man wouldn't put these in till the windy day came, and before he got it all done, his thatch was ruined)

'The man who walked the world said the big road was the short-cut'
(other ways which at first sight appear shorter, may have obstructions we don't know about and may in the end take longer to travel than the high road)

Colmcille's Counsel-
Don't try to govern or improve or correct a person, without reason, for should you do so (it) will be a sin and he will remain your enemy.

Colmcille's Advice-
And that's the true advice
What does not interfere with you
Don't interfere with it.

Monday November 25th 1907
Belfast

Dear Lillie,
        We really loved the American curried eggs recipe you sent. I fried little croutons lightly in a knob of butter and sprinkled them over the top.
I had a look for fish recipes in our new Queen's College book and there are 23 fish recipes in the book. I have sent you the 4 most unusual ones. There is always so much lovely fresh fish for sale in Belfast. I think when the fish is so good you hardly even need a recipe. A lot of the recipes in the book are simple ones like fish cakes, baked stuffed fish and fried cod with a little curried sauce poured over it. There's a recipe from a lady Aunt Annie has met. Laura Beatriz Gullan is from Chile and she's married to the Welsh civil engineer and inventor Hector Freeman Gullan. They live in a big house at Stranmillis in Belfast. Aunt Annie says Hector patented a tram way joint in 1900.
I think you could call Laura's recipe something like "Fish in Bread Nests", but she names it "Fish Pâtés" in the book. I think whoever typed the recipe out must have meant to type Pâtés instead. It is so tasty Lillie and works well with any type of fish.

Fish Pâtés
By L.B. Gullan

Ingredients:
- 225g / 8 oz cold, cooked fish, bones removed
- 28g / 1 oz / ¼ stick butter
- 28g / 1 oz / ¼ cup all-purpose flour
- ¼ pint / 142 ml / 0.6 cups milk
- 3 slices cut from unsliced batch loaf bread, about 4 cm / 1.5 inches thick
- ½ teaspoon salt
- ¼ teaspoon pepper
- well beaten egg to coat bread
- lard for frying

Method:
1. Cut rounds from each slice of bread. Scoop out a little in the centre of each. Brush each with well beaten egg, fry in hot lard, drain.
2. Season the flour with the salt and pepper. Melt butter, add flour and combine. Whisk in the milk and heat to make a thick sauce, whisking all the time.
3. Add flaked fish, beat thoroughly, and pile mixture up in the centre of each round.

Lobster season's just gone, but I thought the next recipe would be a good one to put in our recipe books. It seems like the kind of food that would be popular in big houses like the one where Sophia works. We're lucky to live on an island whose coastline is teeming with fish. Isn't it so sad that just 60 years ago people here didn't have the means to catch all the vast stocks of fish that could have kept them alive when the blight hit the potatoes. Father says the fish off the west coast of Ireland lie far out at sea in very deep water and the small curragh fishing boats were of no use for the big nets needed in deep water fishing. The swell of the Atlantic ocean and the winds which rose up combined to make extreme danger of perishing; the small boats would have so easily been swept against the five hundred feet high cliffs by the edge of the Atlantic.

Lobster Cream
By L. Schneider

Ingredients:
- 1 cooked lobster
- 450g /1 lb whiting, cooked
- 285 ml / 1/2 imperial pint cream, whipped
- 142 ml / 0.6 cups fish stock
- 1 egg
- 40g / 1.5 oz / 1/3 stick butter
- 55g / 2 oz / 1/2 cup plain / all-purpose flour
- salt, pepper, lemon juice and fish sauce
- a drop or two of natural red colouring (if desired)

Method:
1. Rub the whiting through a sieve.
2. Make a roux sauce with the butter, flour and fish stock, season to taste.
3. Blend the roux sauce with the whiting, lemon juice, fish sauce, some of the lobster, shredded, and the egg in a mortar.
4. Fold in the whipped cream. Add a drop or two of natural red colouring at this point, if desired.
5. Butter some dariole moulds, or a soufflé mould, put a little greaseproof paper in the bottom, put in the claws and the nicest parts of the lobster, and then add the soufflé mixture.
6. Cover with greaseproof paper, and steam gently for one hour (1/2 hour for dariole moulds).

Sauce to serve with the Lobster Cream
- 28g/ 1 oz / 1/4 cup plain / all-purpose flour
- 28g / 1 oz / 1/4 stick butter
- 284 ml / 1/2 pint / 1.2 cups fish stock
- 4 x 15 ml tablespoons cream
- salt , pepper & lemon juice to taste

Blend together flour and butter, add stock, and stir till it boils.
Then add cream, salt, pepper and lemon juice.

Fish Gateau
By Mrs Purves

Ingredients:
- 450 g / 1 pound of cooked mixed fish, flaked (smoked cod, haddock, salmon)
- 110 g/ 4 oz / 1/2 cup long grain rice, cooked
- 1dessertspoon chopped parsley (or 1 teaspoon Swiss vegetable Bouillon powder)
- 1/2 teaspoon salt
- 1/4 teaspoon pepper
- 2 eggs
- 28 g /1 oz / 1/8 cup of butter
- 118 mls / 1/2 cup milk

Method:
1. Mix all the dry ingredients together.
2. Beat eggs well, add milk and then the butter, melted.
3. Combine all together and transfer to a buttered mould (or a 2.5 pint/ 1.4 litre ovenproof glass pudding bowl)
4. Cover with tinfoil. Steam for 45 minutes in the oven at approximately 200C / 400F / Gas Mark 6.
5. Turn out and serve with the following sauce poured over it:-

Boiled Mayonnaise Sauce
- 2 yolks of eggs, raw
- 1 teaspoon mustard
- 1 dessertspoon tarragon vinegar
- 1 dessertspoon common vinegar
- 1 dessertspoon salad oil
- 236 mls /1 cup cream
- pepper and salt

1. Beat egg yolks slightly, then add all the ingredients, except for the cream.
2. Beat again, add cream, and boil in a double saucepan, stirring constantly till it thickens.

Cod Curry
by Mrs. Stubbs

Ingredients:
- 450g / 1 lb cod
- 55g / 2 oz / 1/2 stick butter
- 140 ml / 1/4 imperial pint fish stock
- 140 ml / 1/4 imperial pint milk
- 1 teaspoon curry powder
- 25g /1 oz / 1/4 cup plain all purpose flour
- 1 medium sized onion, diced
- juice of half a lemon
- salt and pepper to taste
- a spoonful or two of cream

1. Warm half of the butter in a saucepan. Add the diced onion and fry until golden brown.
2. Stir in the flour and curry powder, add the fish stock and milk; stir till it boils.
3. Put the other half of the butter into a small frying pan, heat and fry the fish (which should be left in large flakes) quickly in it.
4. When lightly browned, lift fish out into the curried sauce, add salt and pepper, cover pan, and simmer very gently over a low heat for 15 minutes. Do not let it boil.
5. If too thick at the last, put in a spoonful of cream. Stir in the lemon juice just before serving.

The remains of many other kinds of cold fish may be used in this way. Boiled rice may be served in a separate dish, or around the fish.

I hope you like the recipes and that all your Christmas wishes and dreams come true Lillie!

With love,
   Eliza

Sunday 1ˢᵗ March 1908
Cavan

Dear Eliza,

        Thanks for writing out all those fish recipes. My book is filling up a bit now. We made the "Fish Gateau" first and it's really tasty.

We've just had a letter from Sophia. The family she works for gave her 10 dollars along with a beautiful dress for Christmas. She says a lot of servant girls she knows just got things like a lace handkerchief for Christmas so she's very lucky to live in such a wealthy household. She's happy, but says she is missing home too. She says the children in the house laugh at the way she says some things. She forgot herself one day and said to the cook that she would go and "wet the tea". She said everyone was in stitches laughing at her. She explained that in Ireland "wetting the tea" means putting the boiling water into the tea leaves to brew, but they still thought it was very peculiar! I'm sending you Mam's recipe for Whiskey Pancakes and Fruit Squares. She just leaves out the whiskey butter for young children and fills them with honey and cream instead.

Whiskey Pancakes

Whiskey Butter:
- 30 ml / 2 tablespoons Irish whiskey
- 28g / 1 oz / 1/4 stick melted butter
- 55g / 2 oz / 1/2 cup powdered (icing) sugar, sieved

Pancake Batter:
- 170g / 6 oz / 1.5 cups self raising flour, sieved 3 times
- 28g / 1 oz / 1/8 cup caster sugar
- a pinch of salt
- 3 large eggs
- 350 ml / 1.5 cups milk
- 15g / 1/2 oz / 1/8 stick melted butter
- 30 ml / 2 tablespoons Irish cream liqueur

Method:
1. First make the whiskey butter by beating the whiskey, icing sugar and melted butter together until smoooth. Set aside in a cool place to set.
2. Put sieved flour, sugar and salt in a bowl.
3. In a separate bowl whisk the eggs lightly with the milk, then mix in to the flour, salt and sugar until smooth.
4. Cover and leave to stand in a cool place for 1 hour.
5. After one hour, combine the gently melted butter with the Irish cream liqueur and mix through the batter.
6. Cook pancakes very thinly on a greased warm griddle or bakestone.
7. Serve with a knob of whiskey butter or honey, and plenty of whipped thick cream.

Fruit Squares

Ingredients:
Pastry
- 225g / 8oz / 2 cups plain flour
- 170g / 6 oz / 1.5 sticks butter
- pinch of salt
- 1 egg
- water to mix
- a little extra sugar to sprinkle on top

Filling:
- 225g / 8 oz / 1.25 cups currants, raisins and sultanas mixed
- 110g / 4 oz / 1/2 cup sugar
- 1 apple
- 1 level teaspoon cinnamon
- 1 level teaspoon mixed spice
- ½ imperial pint / 284mls water
- 1 dessertspoon corn flour / cornstarch

Method:
1. Grease a 30 x 20 cm / 12 x 8 inch Swiss roll tin.

2. To make pastry: Rub margarine into flour until it resembles fine breadcrumbs. Beat egg slightly. Mix egg and a little water into flour mixture to form a stiff dough. Leave in fridge to cool.
3. To make filling: Put fruits, sugar, water and chopped peeled apple in a saucepan. Bring to boil and add mixed spice and cinnamon.
4. Dissolve cornflour in a little cold water and add to saucepan.
5. Boil again until mixture thickens. Allow to cool down.
6. Preheat oven to 200C /400F /Gas Mark 6.
7. Divide pastry in half. Roll out half to cover base of Swiss roll tin and spread fruit filling on top.
8. Cover with other half of the pastry and sprinkle a little sugar across the top. Bake until golden brown. Cut into squares when cold.

Here's another recipe Sophia sent us -

Cabbage With Sausage

Ingredients:
6 sausages
1 large cabbage, very finely shredded
1/2 teaspoon pepper

Method:
Fry the sausages crisp and brown.
Remove sausages from the frying pan and pour off all but 3 tablespoon of the fat.
Put finely shredded cabbage in the frying pan and cook for 6 minutes. Season with pepper.
Arrange in a hot dish and garnish with the sausages.
Serve with mashed potatoes.

I hope you like the recipes Eliza,
                      Love,
                          Lillie

Tuesday March 31st 1908
Belfast

Dear Lillie,

Do you remember the wedding I told you we went to see in Ligoniel? The bride was Violet Villiers Ewart. Well her aunt, who's married to Fred Ewart the linen merchant, has a recipe for chicken and ham pie filling in the Queens College fundraising book. They live in Lambeg, between Belfast and Lisburn, in a large house with several domestic servants working for them. I made this along with Lady Whitla's Vinegar Pastry recipe. Lady Whitla is originally from Staffordshire and met her husband when she was a ward sister in St. Thomas' Hospital. She's friends with Florence Nightingale, and General Booth of The Salvation Army. Her husband Sir William Whitla is from Monaghan and is a brilliant doctor and writer.

Vinegar Pastry
A very old recipe
Lady Whitla

Ingredients:
225g /8 oz / 2 cups plain flour
1 egg
225g / 8 oz / 1 cup butter
2 x 15 ml tablespoons / 30 ml white vinegar

Method:
1. Rub the butter into the flour well.
2. Beat the egg, then mix well with the vinegar, then add to the flour mixture. Handle it as little as possible.
3. Set aside for 2 hours; roll out in very thin layers, and bake in a hot oven.

Chicken and Ham Pie Filling
By Mrs Fred Ewart

Cut up half a cold chicken and 3 slices of cold ham into small pieces.

Sauce:
- 45g / 1.5 oz / 3 x level 15ml tablespoons butter
- 45g / 1.5 oz /1/3 cup plain flour
- 1/4 imperial pint /142 ml milk
- 2 x 15 ml tablespoons cream
- a small bit of chopped onion
- salt and pepper to season

Method:
1. Melt the butter gently, mix in the flour; then whisk in the milk until a smooth sauce is formed.
2. Add the cream and the chopped onion.
3. Season with salt and pepper.
4. Mix the chicken and ham into the sauce and use as a pie filling.

It's been such a wet, cold and windy month. Father says it's a bad start to the year for farm work and all vegetation is very late. Two weeks ago fifteen thousand people watched Ireland play Wales in the Home Nations Rugby Championships at Balmoral Showgrounds here in Belfast. Wales won - they've beaten everyone they played and taken the Triple Crown.

Let me know what you think of the recipes Lillie. I look forward to your letters so much,

    Love,
      Eliza

Saturday April 25th 1908
Cavan

Dear Eliza,

Thanks so much for the recipes. Mam says she'll use Lady Whitla's Vinegar Pastry recipe all the time now. It's really easy and tastes lovely and flaky. Imagine Lady Whitla is a friend of Florence Nightingale. Mam says Florence Nightingale must be nearly 90 years old now!

Sophia has asked Mam to write out how she cooks her fruit. Mam says the proper name for it is Fruit Compote and that it's a different method than just stewing the fruit.

Fruit Compote

In a true fruit compote the syrup must be rich, thick, and well flavoured, the fruit in slices or whole, but in both cases unbroken.
The amount of sugar used is dependent on the acidity of the fruit:-
For acidic fruit
1. Boil 270g / 10 oz /1.33 cups sugar in half an imperial pint / 284 ml of water (or 1/4 pint claret or sherry and ¼ pint water) for 10 minutes. A piece of lemon peel or a cinnamon stick gives flavour depending on the fruit used.
2. Add the fruit and simmer very gently until sufficiently cooked.
3. Carefully lift out the fruit and put it in a dish.
4. Quickly boil the syrup to reduce it in quantity, then pour it over the fruit. A little natural red colouring may also be added.
For sweet fruits use 160g / 6 oz / 3/4 cup of sugar per pound.

It's terribly cold for April. I'm really looking forward to summer this year. Mam and Father are taking us to Auntie Ethel's in Malahide in Dublin. We're to travel by train. Father hasn't seen Auntie Ethel for so long and Mam says the sea air will do us all good. I'll tell you everything when we get back.

Love,
Lillie

Monday June 1ˢᵗ 1908
Belfast

Dear Lillie,

I'm so glad to hear that you're all getting away to the beach. I hope you have a lovely time.

Lillie, I've just had some upsetting news. Tommy is to be married, to a local girl called Helen, who comes from a well to do family. I feel such a silly sad girl, to think that I've wasted so much time dreaming about him. I've just made a batch of éclairs and eaten most of them myself. They have made me feel a bit better though. They were sent into the Queens College recipe book by someone called Miss Duncan. Miss Duncan says in her recipe to use Coombs' flour, and that made me think. Mary Donnelly went over to live with her aunt in Nottingham and got a job as a worker in Coombs' factory there. I've decided to make an application in case they are looking for any more workers. It's time I earned some money, and it's probably time to get away from Belfast. Mrs Donnelly says there's a comfortable mess room with a dressing room, and a large room for recreation and instruction in the factory. She says the place is spotless and "every floor of the factory has lavatories of the most up to date description."

French Pastry for Chocolate Painted Éclairs
Miss J.M. Duncan

Ingredients:
- 284 ml / 1.2 cups water
- 55g / 2 oz / 1/2 stick butter
- 110g / 4 oz / 1 cup Coombs' flour (self-raising flour, sieved 3 times)
- a few drops of vanilla essence
- 2 whole eggs and yolk of one
- 140 ml / ¼ imperial pint double cream (to fill the éclairs)

Method:
1. Preheat oven to a sharp heat between 220C / 425F / Gas Mark 7 and 230C / 450F / Gas Mark 8. Line a baking sheet with greaseproof paper.
2. Put water, butter and flavouring into smooth clean saucepan and boil, then stir in the flour, and cook until it leaves pan clean(around a minute or less.)
3. Remove from the heat, transfer to a basin and beat a few minutes to cool, then drop in yolk of egg, and lastly 2 whole eggs - one at a time beating together all the while until combined.
4. Have ready a piping bag with plain tube fixed, put mixture into bag, and force it through in thin stripes onto baking sheet, and bake for about half an hour, at a very sharp heat for the first 10 minutes, then reduce heat gradually to bake through. Bake until éclairs are dry in the centre. Do not open the oven door for at least the first 15 minutes.
5. Fill with whipped cream and ice with the following icing.

Chocolate Icing

Ingredients:
- 170g / 6 oz / 1 cup icing sugar
- 1 – 2 rounded teaspoons cocoa powder

Method:
Melt chocolate with a little warm water, stir it with icing sugar until smooth, then split pastry, fill with whipped cream and spread chocolate icing over the top.

I hope you like the recipes. I know you warned me when I first told you about Tommy, how daft I was in becoming so infatuated with him!

From a sad Silly-Billy,
      Eliza

Thursday July 2nd 1908
Cavan

Dear Eliza,

Thank you for the éclairs recipe. They taste really delicious. Don't worry yourself over Tommy. Eliza, he isn't the only good man left in the world. I don't think you're silly at all! Have you heard anything from Coombs yet? I think you're so brave to consider going away to England. I hope you'll still write to me if you go there.

Sophia says we should come to America. She has made friends with other housemaids and all the talk is of improving themselves. They all want to work in the great houses with the big purse strings. She says there's a huge demand for good cooks and under-cooks. The big houses pay the best wages, have the best accommodation, and pay the best tips, gifts and other benefits. When you work in one of the big houses they have more servants and so the work is more evenly balanced and you don't tire so easily. The average length of the working day can be as long as fifteen hours in some houses. In the large houses you have more of a chance to specialise. If you land the job of personal attendant to the lady of the house you may even get the chance to travel. Sophia's new friend Bridget travelled to the Spa region in Czechoslovakia and Germany last year. They went to a beautiful area called Vogtland, where Bridget says the air was so sweet and pure she wished she could stay there forever. It was one of Johann Wolfgang von Goethe's favourite places too. Bridget's mistress is a great admirer of Goethe's works. Her favourite saying of his is,

"Hatred is something peculiar. You will always find it strongest and most violent where there is the lowest degree of culture".

Isn't it funny how something said nearly 100 years ago is still so relevant today? Anyway, we're going to Malahide the day after tomorrow. I'm so excited. Could you please send me some more of those recipes from that Belfast Ladies Cook Book?

With love,
Lillie

Saturday 5*th* September 1908
Belfast

Dear Lillie,

Can you believe it – Coomb's have replied to my letter. I'm to start on the fifth of October. Mary Donnelly put in a good word for me and they have offered to give me a chance. I shall be in England for Halloween! I 'm so excited. When you think that mother went all the way to New York when she was only 12, there should be no call for me to feel nervous. But Lillie, I shall miss mother so. I have been sorting through all my childhood books today. I guess I'm not a child any more. I promise to write as often as I can and will send you a letter with my new address as soon as I 'm settled in. Here are some more recipes. Funny you should mention Germany in your last letter. I opened the Queens College cookbook yesterday at a recipe for German biscuits by someone called Mrs Milroy. These biscuits are really popular here in Belfast. I'm not sure if they're really made like this in Germany, but they do taste pretty good. I've added baking powder and a pinch of salt to her recipe because I think it needs them.
It's funny that just last year, Mrs Milroy was using Eiffel Tower Lemonade for her German Biscuits icing in Belfast. Have you ever tasted Eiffel Tower Lemonade? It's the nicest lemonade drink you could ever imagine, made out of lemon crystals, to which you add hot or cold water.

The instructions on the tin say,

"Eiffel Tower Lemonade - For all culinary purposes
Wherever you would use the juice of one lemon, use two medium-sized heaped teaspoons of Eiffel Tower Lemonade Crystals dissolved in 2 tablespoons hot or cold water."

So you could just use lemon juice in this next recipe if you haven't got any Eiffel Tower Lemonade. If you don't like all the lemony flavours in these you can substitute the lemon rind with 5ml / 1 teaspoon of vanilla essence.

When I read Mrs Milroy's recipe it reminded me of the book I got for Christmas 1901 written by Edith Nesbit. In *"The Wouldbegoods"* Oswald, Dora, Dicky, Alice, Noël and H.O. drank Eiffel Tower Lemonade - I looked the story up in my book and it felt like I was 9 years old all over again. I've copied out a little part for you to read too.

"After you go down the lane you come to a cloverfield, and then a cornfield, and then another lane, and then it is the mill. It is a jolly fine mill; in fact- it is two—water and wind ones—one of each kind—with a house and farm buildings as well. I never saw a mill like it, and I don't believe you have either. If we had been in a story-book the miller's wife would have taken us into the neat sanded kitchen where the old oak settle was black with time and rubbing, and dusted chairs for us—old brown Windsor chairs—and given us each a glass of sweet-scented cowslip wine and a thick slice of rich homemade cake. And there would have been fresh roses in an old china bowl on the table. As it was, she asked us all into the parlour and gave us Eiffel Tower lemonade and Marie biscuits."

I wonder has Mrs Milroy read *The Wouldbegoods*...

German Biscuits Recipe
By Mrs Milroy

Ingredients:
- 225g / 8 oz / 2 cups plain all-purpose flour
- 110g / 4 oz / 1/2 cup sugar
- 110g / 4 oz / 1 stick butter
- 1 egg
- 1 level teaspoon baking powder
- a pinch of salt
- 1 level teaspoon grated lemon rind / or 1 teaspoon vanilla essence
- jam or jelly jam to sandwich together

Method:
1. Preheat oven to 350F / 180 C / Gas 4. Line baking trays with baking parchment.

2. Sieve flour, baking powder and salt into a bowl and set aside.
3. In a separate bowl beat the butter and sugar to a cream.
4. Add egg and lemon rind, stir well and gradually beat in the sieved flour.
5. Roll out speedily to about 3mm / 1/8 inch thickness and cut out with a wine glass (or biscuit cutter). Set on lined baking trays and bake for about 10 minutes. Remove from oven and leave to cool on the baking trays.
6. Spread a little jam or jelly on half of the biscuits, place remaining biscuits on top of these. When all are finished, ice and place a glacé cherry on top of each.

For the Icing:
110g / 4 oz / 1 cup icing sugar, moistened with a little hot Eiffel Tower lemonade; beat until smooth.

The wife of the architect who designed St George's market in Belfast gave in this chutney recipe for the new book. She was called Maria Elizabeth White and was born in Cork around the same time as Great-Aunt Sophie, in 1845. Oh Lillie, the sad thing is, she died on 24 February last year, just 3 months before the book was published. It's a really unusual recipe, entitled "Rousham's Royal Bengal Chutney". I wonder where she got it from...

Rousham's Royal Bengal Chutney
By Maria Bretland

Ingredients:
- 675g /1.5 lb/ 5 cups / 6 apples, peeled, cored and cut up (weight after peeling and coring)
- 225g / 8 oz /2 medium onions
- 110g / 4 oz /scant 1/2 cup raisins
- 110g / 4 oz / 0.5 cups light brown sugar
- 110g / 4 oz / 0.5 cups mustard seed
- 28g /1 oz / 1 tablespoon salt (or less, I have halved Maria's salt quantity)
- 28g / 1oz /0.33 cups ground ginger
- 1 tablespoon / 3 cloves garlic, finely chopped
- 28g / 1 oz /0.25 cups cayenne pepper
- 1/2 quart/ 560mls vinegar

Method:
1. Boil the apples, onions and garlic in the vinegar until soft.
2. Stir and mash while boiling; pour over other ingredients, heat through for just a minute or two, then pot as for normal chutney.

I made it yesterday Lillie and there's lots of it. So today I cubed up enough raw chicken for Sam and I, fried it off on the heat, added half a can of plum tomatoes, 85g / 3 oz / 1/4 cup of the chutney , 60ml / 1/4 cup of water, and simmered it for about 45 minutes. I boiled up some rice to go with it and it's the best curry I've ever tasted Lillie.

This Plum Cake recipe is really lovely too. Josiah and Maria's daughter, Norah Madeline Bretland contributed it to the book. I've managed to work out a few exact measurements that needed calculated and added them in for us here. I think it's the Demerara sugar that gives it such a wonderful flavour. You just need to leave the fruit soaking for at least a day and a night in the sherry so that it's well absorbed and not soaking wet.

Plum Cake

Ingredients:
- 675g / 1.5 lb / 6 cups plain all-purpose flour
- 560g / 1.25 lb / 2.7 cups Demerara sugar
- 450g / 1 lb / 4 sticks butter
- 450g / 1 lb / 2.7 cups raisins
- 450g / 1 lb / 2.5 cups currants
- 170g / 6 oz / 1.5 cups candied peel or 160g /6 oz /1 cup glace cherries
- 6 large eggs, at room temperature
- 2 rounded teaspoons mixed spice
- 2 rounded teaspoons baking powder
- 236 ml / 1 cup of sherry

Method:
1. Weigh out fruits, pour sherry over them and leave 24 hours until all the sherry has soaked in and is absorbed. Stir and mix around well several times during soaking period.
2. Grease and line 2 deep round cake tins about 20.5 cm / 8 inches in diameter with a double layer of greased greaseproof paper. Preheat oven to 150C / 300F /Gas Mark 2.
3. Weigh out flour with baking powder and mixed spice and sieve all together once. Set aside.
4. Beat butter and sugar to a cream; add the well beaten yolks of eggs (together with one tablespoon of the weighed out flour to prevent curdling); beat well, add in the rest of the flour, beating all the time. Do not overbeat.
5. Add the whites of eggs, beaten quite stiff; then the fruit, and beat all well together.
6. Put in prepared tins, smooth over top of cakes evenly and bake slowly for 2.5 - 3 hours, reducing temperature to 140C / 275F / Gas Mark 1 if cakes are baking out too fast.
7. Test centre of cakes with a skewer after about 2.5 hours. If the skewer comes out clean they are done.

That's rather a lot of recipes Lillie. I am leaving the book with Mother so that's why I wrote out so many today! I am getting a little nervous about leaving now but I'll just have to get on with it!

Love,
    Eliza

P.S. Granny says when I go away I'm not to forget where I have come from and gave me this poem. It's written by the Dublin poet John Millington Synge.

Prelude

By John Millington Synge

Still south I went and west and south again,
Through Wicklow from the morning till the night,
And far from cities, and the sights of men,
Lived with the sunshine and the moon's delight.

I knew the stars, the flowers, and the birds,
The grey and wintry sides of many glens,
And did but half remember human words,
In converse with the mountains, moors, and fens.

Sunday 6*th* December 1908
Nottingham

Dear Lillie,

I've written my new address on an envelope and put it inside this letter for you. It feels colder here than Belfast, but I'm really growing to love it. The work's hard in the factory but they're pleased with me and I have secured regular employment with Coombs. The factory here is so advanced. The company is called Coombs' "Eureka" Aerated Flour Company. The Eureka flour is put through a sieving machine over 120 times and Mr Coombs adds a secret ingredient to it.

The factory has lots of other products too – we make Coombs' Lady Cake Flour, custard powder, Blanc Mange powder, in lemon, strawberry, pineapple, vanilla, and raspberry flavours, egg powder, Coombs' Light Pastry Powder and Coombs' Malted Food for invalids and young children and a drink called" Coombs' Fruit Saline".

It's good to have Mary Donnelly here to show me my way around on Sundays. The annual Goose Fair was on just a few days after I arrived. The helter skelter sign said "Slip the slip to cure the pip". I didn't know what "the pip" meant but Mary says "having the pip" means being in a huff or sulking. It's great fun to learn new sayings that we don't have at home.

Mary Donnelly says a baker from Mayo is coming next spring time to help develop new products. She says Coombs is a really good company which has grown very fast. She's heard a rumour that the owners are under a lot of pressure and they are pinning their hopes on the new baker next spring.

Everyone is football mad here. Lots of the lads go to watch Nottingham Forest when they are playing at home on a Saturday. Mary says they're playing Millwall in February. Her friend Frank is a big Millwall fan.

Lillie there's so much going on here I haven't even had time to think about our recipe books. I hope you have a wonderful Christmas and please write soon,

    Love,
        Eliza

Monday 4th January 1909
Cavan

Dear Eliza,

I'm so glad to hear that everything's going so well in Nottingham. I'm really looking forward to hearing more about it there. Now I'm getting letters from England and The States I do feel sometimes like I'm letting my life pass by sitting here in Cavan reading about everyone else. But I couldn't do it to Mam I don't think...

I nearly forgot to tell you; we had such a lovely time when we visited Auntie Ethel in Malahide last summer. She has book cases lined with books from the floor to the ceiling. She told me I could take as many books as I wanted to bring home with me. I spent most of my time reading when I was there ,but only took a few books as I didn't like to be greedy.

One of the books which she let me take home was "*Fairy & Folk Tales of the Irish Peasantry*", compiled by William Butler Yeats in 1888. There's a brilliant story in it by William Carleton called "*The Pudding Bewitched*". It's about a pudding that escapes from its pot and is chased by a crowd of religious bigots who all want to take a dig at it. Mam says Carleton wasn't afraid to paint a realistic picture of people as they really are, but maybe that's why he never made much money. Maybe he'd have earned more if he had been a bit two-faced and didn't always say what he really thought. Anyhow, it was so funny I read it three times. I laughed until I could laugh no more. William Carleton could write each word of the local tongue so well you could almost see the people and feel that small-minded, mean-spiritedness that eats up some people so much. It's quite a long story to write out and the words are spelt just as the people said them. It'll take me ages, but I'll write it out for you and send it to you whenever I get it all done.

We had a lovely Christmas. Aunt Margaret came to stay and Mam was so glad to see her. She told us all about summertime in Donegal. She's been working in a guest-house there for the last few years. The regular customers are so fond of her now that she gathers up a lot of extra money in tips; so much last year that she decided to stay in style in an inn for one night on her way back home.

She stopped off in Belleek and spent the night in the little hotel there. She asked the proprietor if he had any eels left in his tank and whether he would let her have some for dinner. He went out right away to catch the fish and it was cooked for the "table d'hote "dinner that evening.

She managed to get the recipe from the chef (well I've told you before what Aunt Margaret's like!)The Harvey's sauce is best made at least 2 weeks in advance! Aunt Margaret says the chef is one of the best cooks she has ever met. I hope you like it. Please write soon, I can't wait to hear all your news,

Love,
    Lillie

Fresh Water Eel Pie

Ingredients;
- 2 eels
- 55g /2 oz / 1/2 stick butter
- 240ml / 1 cup of sherry
- 120ml /1/2 cup of Harvey's sauce (next recipe)
- 6 mushrooms, chopped
- 1 shallot, chopped
- bunch of parsley
- 28g / 1 oz / 1/4 cup cornflour / corn starch
- 1/2 a lemon
- 3 eggs, hard boiled and cut into quarters
- seasonings – nutmeg & cayenne
- rich pastry for the pie crust

Method:
1. Cleanse and prepare 2 good-sized eels in the normal manner.
2. Cut them in 3 inch lengths and put them in a stew pan with the fresh butter, sherry and Harvey's sauce. Add barely enough water to cover.
3. Next add the chopped mushrooms, parsley, pepper, salt, nutmeg, and the chopped shallot.
4. Bring to the boil, then take out the pieces of eel and put them in a pie dish.
5. Thicken the sauce with the cornflour and stir till it boils.

6. Add lemon juice and cayenne, then pour the sauce over the eels in the pie dish.
7. Cover this with the quartered hard boiled eggs.
8. Roll out the pastry to form a pie crust.
9. Bake for about 1 hour at 190C / 375F / Gas Mark 5 and serve hot or cold.

Harvey's Sauce

Ingredients:
- 475 ml / 2 cups strong vinegar
- 6 anchovies
- 2 heads garlic (all the cloves in 2 garlic bulbs)
- 90ml 2/5 cup soy sauce
- 90 ml / 2/5 cup mushroom ketchup
- 1.5tsps cayenne pepper
- red food colouring

Method:
1. Mash and dissolve the anchovies in the vinegar then stir in the soy sauce, mushroom ketchup and cayenne pepper.
2. Divide the garlic cloves, peel and then chop them finely before adding to the vinegar mix.
3. Add a few drops of red colouring then put into a large, sterilized jar.
4. Leave to infuse in the vinegar for 2 weeks, shaking each day.
5. At the end of this time strain the liquid and pour into sterilized bottles with air-tight corks.

Sunday 27ᵗʰ June 1909
Nottingham

Dear Lillie,

I'm so sorry I haven't written in so long. Each week flies by so fast here. The factory is so busy. Danny the new baker has arrived from Mayo. He has lovely brown curly hair which he wears in a quiff down over his forehead. He's very handsome in a rustic sort of way and very serious about his work. He disappears with Mr Coombs and no one knows much about him. All the girls are wondering how long he's going to be staying.

How's everyone in Cavan? Have you heard from Sophia lately? I hope everything's well with you all. Are you still writing your recipes into your book? I've made friends with a girl called Emily who went to the "National Training School of Cookery" in London. Some of her recipes are printed in a cookbook she has. The book is called *"Isobel's Home Cookery"*. She makes some fabulous food, and I think I will slowly be able to get the recipes from her. I'll send them to you as I get them. Here are two she gave me last week.

Gooseberry and Almond Tartlets

Ingredients:
450g / 1 lb ripe red gooseberries
55g / 2 oz / 1/4 cup sugar
110g / 4 oz / scant cup blanched and chopped almonds
rich rough puff pastry
some flaked pistachio nuts to decorate
extra caster sugar to sweeten
whipped cream to decorate

Method:
1. Stew a pound / 450g of ripe red gooseberries with 2 oz / 55g / 1/4 cup of sugar till tender.
2. Mix almonds into the fruit.
3. Line some patty pans with rich puff pastry and heap a spoonful of the mix

into the centre of each.
4. Dust with caster sugar and bake in a medium hot oven for 20 minutes.
5. Sprinkle with chopped pistachio nuts and place a tiny cap of whipped cream over each.

Apple Amber Pudding

Ingredients:
enough shortcrust pastry to line a pie dish
6 large apples
55g / 2 oz / 1/2 stick butter
55 g / 2 oz / 1/4 cup sugar
the thin rind of 1 lemon
3 eggs, separated
some caster sugar
glace cherries and angelica for decoration

Method:
1. Line a pie dish with shortcrust pastry.
2. Peel core and slice the apples. Place them in a pan with the butter ,sugar and rind of lemon, and stew slowly till tender.
3. Rub through a sieve and cool slightly. Beat yolks of two or three eggs thoroughly, and add to the sieved apple mixture, mixing in well.
4. Pour all into lined pie dish and bake at 350F / 180C / Gas Mark 4 for about 20 minutes.
5. Whip the whites of the eggs till stiff, pile these over the baked pie .sift a little white sugar over, decorate the edges of the whipped eggs with pre-served cherries and strips of Angelica.
6. Place the pudding in a cool oven 300F / 150 C / Gas Mark2 to set the meringue and tinge it a delicate brown.

I do miss home and keep thinking how hard it must be for Sophia in The States. I hope you like Emily's recipes Lillie. Please write soon,

Love,
Eliza

Wednesday 1st September 1909
Cavan

Dear Eliza,
      Thanks for your letter and the lovely recipes. Our recipe books are going to be far more interesting than we ever imagined when we started writing them. It seems like they've taken a life of their own now as I read back over the last five years of our little book.
It's been such a cool summer here this year; the poor weather just seems to go on and on, and it's all everyone talks about at the minute. Aunt Minnie has gone off to work for a family called the Drews in County Waterford. Henry Drew is a retired doctor and has moved back here with his family and wife Cherry to Mocollup Castle. They've even brought their South African cook with them. She's called Antge van der Berg and is twenty-three years old. Including Aunt Minnie they have five domestic servants. A local man called Patrick Healy is their coachman. He's twenty eight years old.
Aunt Minnie says a friend of Mrs Cherry Drew's called Elizabeth is putting together a cookbook. Elizabeth lives in Augher Castle in County Tyrone. She was Elrington before she married John Carmichael Ferrall in Dublin in 1899. Her husband is the son of John Jervais O'Ferrall Carmichael Ferrall who died 5 years ago. Her husband's great grandfather was Sir Hugh Lyle Carmichael. She knows lots of people round the country Eliza.
Aunt Minnie has offered to help her with the lay-out of the recipes for the book; so Aunt Minnie is going to send them to me as they come in. I can't tell anyone but I shall send them on to you for your book. Just keep them to yourself until Mrs Carmichael Ferrall's book is published. Here is Mrs Drew's contribution for the new book and another from a Mrs Betty.

An Apple Hedgehog
(Good for children)
Mrs Drew, Mocollup Castle, Co. Waterford

1. Bake 3 or 4 apples until they feel soft when you pinch them.
2. Cut blanched almonds into 4 (or use flaked almonds) to form spines.
3. Place apples close together on a dish, and stick almonds thickly all over the apples.
4. Cover with a rich sweet custard or whipped cream.

Strawberry or Raspberry Whip
Mrs Rowland Betty, Aughnacloy

Ingredients:
- 1 cupful fresh fruit such as strawberries or raspberries
- 1 cupful sugar
- White of 1 egg

Method:
Beat all together for 10 or 12 minutes, and serve with whipped cream.

Isn't writing out all these recipes so much fun? These recipe must be the easiest ones yet!

Love,
    Lillie

Narrator: Raw egg can be dangerous to babies and toddlers, elderly people pregnant women and people who are already unwell.
Using pasteurised eggs minimises this risk, because the pasteurisation process kills salmonella. When using raw egg be sure that it comes from hens have been vaccinated against salmonella, otherwise use pasteurised egg white.

Sunday March 27th 1910
Nottingham

Dear Lillie,

      Sorry it's taken me so long to write back to you. Something really exciting has happened. Some of the lads brought some mistletoe into the factory before Christmas and put it up in the mess room. Everyone was fooling around and in the middle of it all Danny kissed me under the mistletoe. To make a long story short, we are now courting. Lillie, I feel so giddy all the time. I have butterflies in my stomach. He's such a strong, clever person. He knows everything about baking. I haven't told him about our recipe books yet in case he would think me silly.

He tells me he used to spend every spare minute in the garden growing vegetables back home in Mayo. After work each day he would go straight out to plant and weed everything. He says he started off with just a few drills of potatoes. Now he has herbs, carrots, cabbage and rhubarb. His mother is looking after it all now he is away. He used to take the vegetables to the local shop on the back of his bicycle. He saved every shilling he got and plans to start his own bakery someday.

I'm going to keep writing up my recipe book anyhow. Who knows, maybe sometime I will show him it! Have you got any more recipes from that new book Aunt Minnie is helping out with?

Danny seems to have forgotten home a little and is always making plans. He's very ambitious and talks of New Zealand, Australia and Canada. He's taking me to Nottingham's new picture house "The Victoria Electric Palace" next Saturday. I can't wait! I hope you've had a lovely Easter too.

                                                                 Love,
                                                                 Eliza

P.S. Here's two more of Emily's recipes.

Steamed Rhubarb

1. Clean the rhubarb and cut it into 2 inch lengths.
2. Set it in a stewing jar or basin along with a nice piece of lemon rind. Do not add any water to it.
3. Cook in a steamer over boiling water until nearly tender.
4. Add sugar to taste, return to the steamer and cook for a quarter of an hour.

Emily says rhubarb cooked like this will be a nice deep pink colour and of excellent flavour.

Cinnamon biscuits

Ingredients:
- 450g / 1 pound / 4 cups flour
- 225g / half a pound / 1 stick butter
- 1 egg
- 40g / 1.5 oz / 8 level teaspoons ground cinnamon
- halved almonds

Method:
1. Preheat the oven to 350F / 180C / Gas Mark 4.
2. Mix the butter and sugar well together, add the egg and cinnamon, and lastly the flour, which should be very slowly stirred in to prevent lumps. Roll right thin and cut into rounds and put half an almond on top of each biscuit.
3. Bake for approximately 10 minutes.
4. Turn upside down to cool. They should be very crisp.

Thursday 2nd June 1910
Cavan

Dear Eliza,

I'm so happy to hear your news. It sounds like you're falling in love with Danny. I hope all your dreams come true Eliza. I wish we had a cinema in Cavan. Maybe we'll get one soon. I wish I had someone to love too Eliza. Aunt Minnie has sent another recipe – this one comes from a Dublin family. Emily Elizabeth Maude Heard is married to General Practitioner Dr. Robert Lynn Heard and they have 8 children.

We tried first making it with raisins, the way Mrs Heard had written the recipe out. It was grand on the day we made it but by the next day it had dried out a bit. So we sliced it really thinly and spread butter on it. Aunt Minnie says in such a large family full of children, parents, a governess and 2 servants, there would be barely a crumb left of that cake after supper! Mrs Heard probably doesn't realise what happens it the day afterwards as it has all been cleared by everyone! I did notice that the fruit didn't sink at all so I made another one and replaced the raisins with glacé cherries. It worked perfectly and the cherries made it that little bit more moist. I am so happy because I never could get cherries to stay up in a cake until now. In fact I would say this is the best cherry cake recipe ever. I hope you enjoy it too!

Looking forward to hearing from you soon,

Love,

Lillie

Cherry Cake

Ingredients:
- 450g / 1 lb / 4 cups plain all-purpose flour
- 450g / 1 lb / 2 cups glacé cherries (or make a fruit cake with juicy raisins)
- 225g / 8 oz / 2 sticks butter
- 225g / 8 oz / 1 cup caster sugar
- 2 rounded teaspoons baking powder
- 4 large eggs

Method:
1. Rub the butter into the flour, add the fruit and other dry ingredients.
2. In a separate bowl beat the eggs well.
3. Add these to the dry ingredients and mix.
4. Put into a greased and lined round cake tin 23 x 7 cm / 9 x 3 inch, and bake for around 2 hours in a very moderate oven about 150C / 300F /Gas Mark 2 until a skewer inserted into the centre comes out clean.

Narrator: General Practitioner Dr. Robert Lynn Heard was one of the survivors of the wreck of "The Ceres" at Carnsore in 1866. 29 passengers and 9 crew died when "The Ceres" cargo and passenger steamship came aground about a mile west of Carnsore Point in Co. Wexford back on 10th November 1866. Robert was the only child saved and his mother Ellen the only woman on board saved. Robert's grandfather, Richard Griffith Noble Heard, (Chief Inspector of the Coastguards) and Robert's father, also called Dr Robert Lynn Heard, who was born in Donaghadee in County Down, both survived. Emily's husband, then only 10 months old, was given up for dead, only to be rescued some hours later by a sailor, who had been tempted by Robert's grandfather's offer of £5 to anyone who would bring the child ashore.
This little boy grew up, got married in his late twenties and he and his wife Emily had 8 children. Their address was "Carnsore" Monkstown, Dublin.

Sunday 31ˢᵗ July 1910
Nottingham

Dear Lillie,

I still haven't told Danny about our recipe books but I did tell him the story about the wreck of the Ceres. I said that you had sent me Mrs Heard's fruitcake recipe. He told me one of his secrets to good fruitcake. He says you must soak all the dried fruit first for several hours. Then you must drain it well and dry it. This reconstitutes the fruit and makes for a moister cake. That's why the cake was so dry when you made it with raisins. Here is Emily's recipe for Rhubarb Jam:

Rhubarb Jam

1. For every pound of fruit allow one pound of sugar and one lemon.
2. Finely shred the peel of the lemon into julienne strips. Squeeze the juice from the lemon and strain.
3. Put the sugar into a preserving pan with a little water, and bring to the boil. Skim frequently to clear of any substance that forms on the surface.
4. When it has reduced to a thick syrup, which on dropping a little into cold water becomes hard, add the peel and juice of the lemon.
5. Colour rather deeply with red food colouring and stir continually to prevent burning.
6. The jam will take about one hour's boiling. Test a little on a plate - it is ready when it sets sufficiently. Pot in the usual way.

Emily seems to add red colouring to all her rhubarb recipes! It does make it extra nice looking. She gave me this lovely soup recipe which she learnt at cooking school too.

Cressy or French Carrot soup

- 6 carrots, sliced
- one head of celery, chopped small
- 110 g / ¼ lb raw ham
- 55g / 2 oz / 1/2 stick butter
- 1650 ml / 7 cups Stock or water
- 140 ml / 0.6 cups cream
- 2 onions, sliced
- cayenne and salt to season

Method:
1. Put carrots, celery and onions into a stew pan.
2. Add ham and butter.
3. Put the lid on the stew pan and simmer the contents for 10 minutes, then add two-thirds of the stock, and cook very slowly until all the vegetables are tender.
4. Drain off the stock into a jug, pound the vegetables, add back the stock they were cooked in plus the remaining third of the stock.
5. Purée or sieve. Return the soup to the stew pan, and stir until it boils.
6. Then stand of the heat and let the grease rise, which then must be skimmed off with a wooden spoon. Let the soup just simmer for a quarter of an hour, add cream, a seasoning of cayenne and salt, and serve with fried dice of bread.

Danny's still talking about going to Australia. I hope he doesn't. It's hard to tell what's in his head sometimes. I can still hear Granny's wistful dreaming, "When I walk with you I feel as if I had a flower in my buttonhole". She talks like it was Grandpa saying it but Mother says it's from Thackeray. I wish I could make Danny feel like that. He's so reserved and I can't quite tell what he's really thinking. I've fallen in love with him but it's hard to tell how much he really cares for me. He's ever so practical and more concerned with getting on and how people think of him. Surely the people closest to us should be the ones that matter most?

      Love,
      Eliza

Tuesday 30th August 1910
Cavan

Dear Eliza,

We're all fine here and having a lovely summer. July was nice and sunny but it's cooler now and the days are shortening in already.

Thanks for the tip about the rhubarb. It really does help, especially if the rhubarb stalks aren't looking their best red. I've tried it in rhubarb crumbles and pies and everyone seems to imagine they taste better than normal; without realizing all I have done is add a little more colour! Father says taking large quantities of rhubarb is bad for the kidneys but small amounts of rhubarb are actually good for you. It's strange how the leaves of the rhubarb are poisonous. We have ours well away from where any animals can reach them. Aunt Minnie has sent a lovely recipe for chocolate cake. She's not sure who Miss M'Dowell is. Apparently this cake keeps well, but chocolate cake never lasts more than a day or two in our house so I never had the chance to find out if that is true or not! The icing recipe arrived with no name, just the letter "E" ! The sandwich cake is from a lady whose husband is a drapery salesman.

Really Good Chocolate Cake
By Miss E. M'Dowell

Ingredients:

225g / 8oz / 2 cups all-purpose plain flour, sieved
225g / 8 oz / 2 sticks butter or margarine
225g / 8 oz / 1 cup caster sugar, sieved
225g / 8 oz / 2 x 4 ounce bars milk chocolate, grated, then melted
110g / 4 oz / 1 cup ground almonds
7 eggs at room temperature
1 heaped teaspoon of Sal Volatile (baking powder)

Method:
1. Grease and line a 23cm x 7 cm / 9 inch spring form cake tin.
2. Beat the butter or margarine to a cream.
3. Beat the yolks of 7 eggs into this, and beat in the melted, grated chocolate.
4. Add the sieved flour and the sieved sugar, ground almonds and raising agent.
5. Beat up the whites of the eggs to form stiff peaks and add them.
6. Bake in a slow oven 300-325F / 150-160C / Gas Mark 2 - 3 for 1 – 1.5 hours or until baked through. Remove from tin and set on a cooling rack.

Miss M'Dowell advises "This cake keeps well, and is better if kept for 10 days."

Chocolate Icing
By "E"
Ingredients:
- 85g / 3 oz of milk chocolate
- 60ml / 1/4 cup of boiling water
- approx 170g / 6 oz / 1 cup of sieved icing sugar

Method:
1. Grate milk chocolate into boiling water.
2. Mix well until melted then set aside to cool.
3. When it has cooled gradually add sieved icing sugar. When the right consistency to coat the back of a wooden spoon is reached, pour over cake.

Sandwich Cake
by Mrs Annie M'Cavery, Edenmore, Coleraine

Ingredients:
- 2 eggs
- the weight of one in sugar and the weight of one in flour
- a little milk (about 30 ml)
- a teaspoon of baking powder

Method:
1. Beat eggs and sugar for 15 minutes, then add flour gradually, then the milk and baking powder.
2. Bake in a hot oven 220C / 425F / Gas Mark 7 for 5 to 7 minutes.

Elizabeth wants to have lots of little sayings mixed through the recipes in her book. Here's two that have arrived already. A Miss Day from Bishop's Court in Clones sent in this one written by Kathleen J. Edgar.

"Smile awhile
and while you smile, another smiles -
And soon there's miles and miles of smiles
and Life's worth while Because you Smile."

O'Hanlon of Orior, Innishannon, Co. Cork sent in a Walt Whitman quote -

"Keep your face always towards the sunshine, and the shadows will fall behind you"

Everyone here is talking of how Belfast is so busy at the moment with the building of the Olympic and Titanic liners. The Olympic is to be ready next year and the Titanic the year after. The boys are all talking about emigration and I think father just wants to get us girls married off as soon as possible. Well he needn't think I will just marry someone to please him. I would sooner never marry than be stuck with someone I didn't love, or who didn't love me.
Sophia has met a lovely fellow from Kilmore in County Fermanagh. It's funny how she should go all the way to New York only to meet someone from down the road. It sounds like she has fallen head over heels in love. Maybe if I were to go away I might fall in love too. How are you and Danny getting on?
Looking forward to your next letter,
      Love,
       Lillie

Christmas 1910
Nottingham

Dear Lillie,

I hope you're having a lovely Christmas in Cavan. It's magical here in Nottingham. Danny has given me a beautiful bracelet of gold hearts. He even told me he loves me but then a few minutes later it seemed like he wished he hadn't said that. Do you think that's just the way men are Lillie?
He took me to the picture house to see "Tilly the Tomboy Visits the Poor". He didn't seem much impressed by it until the part where "They Take Refuge in a Bakehouse" came on. The tomboy girls run riot in a bakery and there's flour everywhere. He laughed so much he nearly cried. I liked the set "The Tomboys Annex a Motor Van". The girls steal a laundry van and throw the laundry out over the top of those chasing them. It would be great if you could hear what they were saying, though the musical accompaniment by the pianist was lovely to listen to.
Mother has made another recipe out of the Queen's College book that I left at home. It's pretty nice and reminds me a little of that pineapple pudding recipe Miss Porter gave Sophia when she was leaving for America.

Banana Pudding
By M.E. Rea

Pastry ingredients for lining pie dish:
- 55 g /2 oz / 1/2 cup plain all-purpose flour
- 28g / 1 oz / 1/4 stick butter
- a pinch of baking powder
- a spoonful of milk to bind

Pastry Method:
1. Weigh out flour and baking powder into a bowl. Rub butter in finely until all resemble fine breadcrumbs. Add a few drops of milk, just enough to bind pastry together.
2. 2. Grease an ovenproof pie dish of around 22 cm /8.5 inch in size. Roll the pastry out thinly on a floured worktop.
3. Line base and sides of dish with pastry.

Filling Ingredients:
- 4 - 6 bananas
- 1 heaped tablespoon of sugar
- 1 tablespoon of lemon juice or sherry

Custard Batter Ingredients:
- 40g / 1.5 oz / 2/5 stick butter
- 55g / 2 oz / 1/2 cup plain all-purpose flour
- 1 heaped dessertspoon sugar
- 568 ml / 1 imperial pint milk
- 1 teaspoon vanilla essence
- 2 eggs – keep the white of one of these separate for meringue later
- 55g / 2 oz / 1/4 cup caster sugar for meringue topping

Method:
1. Melt butter, blend in the flour, add milk, sugar and vanilla, and stir till it thickens and boils, whisking all the time.
2. Remove from heat, add in 1 whole egg and 1 egg yolk and mix well.
3. Slice the bananas and arrange across the pastry base. Sprinkle with sugar and lemon juice and pour the custard batter over the bananas.
4. Bake at 200C / 400F / Gas Mark 6 for 20 – 25 minutes, then lower heat and bake for another 15-20 minutes.
5. Remove from oven and lower oven heat to 140C / 275F / Gas Mark 1.
6. Whip reserved egg white until it forms peaks. Add the 55g / 2 oz / 1/4 cup caster sugar and whip again.
7. Transfer this meringue mixture to a piping bag fitted with a nozzle, and pipe neatly starting from the centre of the pudding working outwards. Leave an unpiped border around the edge.

8. Put back in the oven and bake for 10 to 15 minutes or until meringue starts to crisp.

They even taught some Irish recipes at the National Cooking school in London. Emily says she even learnt Danish, French and German recipes there too.

Emily's Irish Carrageen Moss Jelly
(If the slightly bitter taste of which this moss possesses is objected to, it may be partially removed by adding a pinch of bicarbonate of soda to the water in which it is soaked.)
1. Wash the moss well in several waters and soak for half an hour.
2. To make a jelly, boil an ounce of Moss in 2 Imperial pints / 1100 ml / 4.7 cups of water for six hours, until reduced to about half the quantity, strain and leave to cool.
3. If pouring into a mould, sweeten with caster sugar, and add the juice of a lemon, with powdered cinnamon, or any other flavouring preferred.
4. Melt and mix, then turn into a wet mould and leave to set.

Emily's Irish Oatcakes
These are really easy to make and much superior to the machinemade oatcakes available in the shops.
1. Put three or four handfuls of oatmeal in a bowl, add a small piece of salted butter the size of a walnut. Pour nearly boiling water over and mix with your hand until the oatmeal is all moistened. It must not be made too wet.
2. When thoroughly moulded sprinkle a little dry oatmeal over, turn out on the baking board, and mould out with the back of the fingers until a thin cake is formed. Then cut into quarters, and bake on a griddle until firm. Do not let the griddle become too hot these are delicious served with chutneys and cheese at any meal.

How's that recipe book of Elizabeth's coming on? Who knows Lillie, maybe someday we could publish our own recipe books!

Love,
Eliza

Thursday February 2nd 1911
Cavan

Dear Eliza,

I'm so happy to hear that all is going so well with you and Danny. Aunt Minnie is sending me recipes thick and fast - here is one from the Carmichael Ferralls' butler in Augher Castle!

Duchess Pudding
By Alexander Montgomery

Ingredients:
- 3 eggs
- their weight in sugar
- the weight of 2 in self-raising flour
- 110g / 4 oz / 1 stick soft butter
- slices of citron
- a handful of currants

Method:
1. Butter a pudding bowl well and place slices of citron at the bottom.
2. Drop a handful of currants into the centre of the bowl.
3. Beat remainder of ingredients together, then pour in the mixture, and steam for 1.5 hours.

Imagine living in a beautiful castle overlooking a little lake and having a butler who made puddings like that Eliza!

Elizabeth has decided to put a section in the book entitled "Household Hints". A lady called Mrs Gumbleton from Twyning Manor in Tewkesbury has sent some hints for the book. Aunt Minnie says she was born in Newfoundland. I wonder what brought her to England. Here is one of the hints she sent in:
"Filleted plaice or sole is much more delicious in flavour if baked instead of fried. Put a small piece of butter on each fillet".

When I read that it reminded me of cooking fish over the fire down by the Annalee River on late summer evenings. I can't wait for summertime again Eliza.

Rev. J. Winter, who lives near Augher Castle in County Tyrone, has given Elizabeth this home-cure recipe for rheumatism.

Domestic Remedy For Rheumatism

"Pour 1 pint / 560 ml water on a teaspoonful of celery seed; keep hot on tripod by fire (or over a low heat) and drink it at intervals during the day until cured."

I'll write again as soon as I get more recipes from Aunt Minnie.

Love,
Lillie

Narrator: Rev. Winter's home-cure recipe was a good one. 21st century natural remedy practitioners are agreed on the benefits of celery seed in helping to treat rheumatoid arthritis, fybromyalgia and high blood pressure. It's all down to a compound known as 3-nbutylphthalide, or 3nB.
3nB is unique to celery and is what gives celery it's characteristic flavour and smell.

Sunday 2nd April 1911
Nottingham

Dear Lillie,

Thank you for the butler's pudding recipe. I'm always wondering whose recipe is coming next. That's really sweet of the butler to give his recipe. It sounds like he's just part of the family in that castle.
When I read what you wrote about the fish it made me miss home. Danny has told me that the factory is in trouble. They've expanded at such a rapid pace that they are finding it difficult to sustain everything. One of the directors has told this to Danny in confidence. None of the workers in the factory are to know, as they are still hoping to turn the whole thing round.
He has promised to help Danny find employment elsewhere, and has friends in New York whom he can write to if Danny is interested. Danny says he has to tell him to go ahead as he's lucky even to get such an offer of help. He still doesn't say much about his feelings for me. You know Lillie, this means I may be jobless and jilted at the same time! Danny hasn't asked me to come with him and just talks of going to New York in the singular. I'm trying not to think at the moment but I can't even sleep right I'm so distressed.
Granny always said when you're worried make sure you keep really busy. That way you don't have time to think about the problem. I've been trying to do this but it's all still in my head no matter what I do. Emily knows there's something wrong with me but I can't tell her what it is. I just have to keep off the subject of Danny and talk about food to her. She gave me this recipe for Mushroom Pie the other day.

Mushroom Pie

Ingredients:
- mushrooms, stalks removed and kept aside
- some breadcrumbs
- a little corn flour / corn starch
- butter and cream
- seasonings
- short crust pastry

Method:
1. Butter a pie dish and then line it with short paste, rolled very thin.
2. Scatter breadcrumbs over the bottom of the dish, then a deep layer of mushrooms (keep the stalks for later).
3. Season them with salt and pepper and a few little pieces of butter.
4. Scatter a 1.25 cm / half inch layer of breadcrumbs over the top.
5. Cover with pastry as you would for any other pie. Make a hole in the centre of the crust and bake in a hot oven.
6. While the pie is cooking, stew the mushroom stalks in a little water, with salt and pepper added to flavour. Strain, thicken with flour and add 4 x 15ml tablespoons of cream and keep warm.
7. When the pie is cooked remove it from the oven, and pour the sauce through a funnel into the centre of the pie. Serve hot.

I'm surrounded by people who love preparing food and who think about food more than they think about anything else Lillie. Back home it was always Granny and her poetry ringing in my ears. Here it's either Emily or Danny talking and planning out dreams about food every day. I listen to them and think of our recipe books Lillie. Baking and cooking is so much fun, but it all feels a little bitter sweet to me at the moment. I just can't seem to keep my mind on anything other than Danny going away now.
Thank you for listening to all my woes Lillie. I hope all is well with you all in Cavan,
   Love,
     Eliza

Narrator:

History of Coombs' Flour

Coomb's 'Eureka' Aerated Flour Company Ltd was established in 1885 by a Mr W.A. Coombs in Nottingham, England. The modern, purpose-built five-storey factory produced various flour products and dried egg powder.
The company was awarded numerous medals at exhibitions, including a gold medal at a Cookery Exhibition at the Imperial Institute in London in 1896, and a Gold at the Brussels International Exhibition in 1897.
In spite of much success and excellent products, the company began to struggle financially in 1909. A notice in the London Gazette of 14 December 1909 announced 'In the Matter of COOMBS' "EUREKA" AERATED FLOUR COMPANY Limited and Reduced; and in the Matter of the Companies (Consolidation) Act, 1908' stating 'Notice is hereby given ... that the capital of the company be reduced from £25,000 to £11,666. 13s. 4d.'
By 1913, the London Gazette of 15 August announced 'In the matter of the Companies (Consolidation) Act 1908 and of COOMBS' "EUREKA" AERATED FLOUR COMPANY Limited (in voluntary liquidation) Notice is hereby given that a general Meeting of the above named company will be held at 2, St. Peter's Church Walk, Nottingham on Wednesday the 17th day of September 1913 at 11 o'clock in the forenoon, for the purpose of having the liquidator's accounts, showing the manner in which the winding-up has been conducted and the property of the Company disposed of, laid before such meeting, and of hearing any explanation that may be given by the Liquidator, and also of determining, by Extraordinary Resolution, the manner in which the books, accounts and documents of the Company and of the Liquidator thereof, shall be disposed of.
Dated this 6th day of August 1913. Arthur J. Chamberlain, liquidator.'

Tuesday 20ᵗʰ June 1911
Cavan

Dear Eliza,
      I don't know what to say in reply to your news. It sounds like you may be coming back home after all, unless you end up going to New York with Danny. Oh Eliza, I hope everything sorts out for the best for you. Harland and Wolff in Belfast plan to launch the "Olympic" before next winter. It'll be the largest passenger vessel in the world Eliza. They say the "Titanic" will be even bigger!

I hope you have a great summer in Nottingham. We have had a lovely long dry spell here but father is hoping for rain. He says the ground needs it!

Thinking of you and wishing everything best in the world for you,

Love,
    Lillie

PS Two of the old Irish sayings Sophia sent me might help you be strong right now -

"Speak to misfortune only when you meet it"

"There are fish in the tide as good as any that have been taken"

Sunday 6th August 1911
Nottingham

Dear Lillie,

Thank you so much for your letter and kind words. The directors in the factory have written to their business acquaintances in New York. Danny is just waiting on any news from them. He is working very hard at the factory, trying I think, to avoid the unavoidable. The factory is such a great place to work. We make some of the best products in England. I hope the factory will survive.

Emily knows I am not myself, and tries everything to cheer me up. She made the most beautiful cake the other day. It was two really light sponge cakes sandwiched together with a thin layer of raspberry jam. The only bit of the recipe she would give me was the icing:

Icing for Coconut Sandwich Cake

1. Weigh out 110g / 4 oz / 2/3 cup icing sugar. Mix a little water with rose water and add just enough to the icing sugar to make a smooth paste.

2. Spread on top of the cake with a broad knife dipped into cold water. While the icing is still soft, sprinkle with desiccated or grated coconut. Leave it for a short time in the kitchen heat to harden.

I still haven't told Danny about our recipe books. There is something quite therapeutic about keeping them, but I'm not sure what he will make of mine if I tell him. His creations and recipes are all so advanced and commercial I don't know what he would think of ours. Hope everyone is keeping well in Cavan. I look forward to all your letters Lillie,

Love,

Eliza

Monday 2nd October 1911
Cavan

Dear Eliza,

What a long hot summer we have had here in Ireland. Father was so glad when it rained in the middle of September. We picked huge basins full of blackberries and have made lots of blackberry jelly for winter. I've even managed a sun-tan this year.

Eliza, I've just got the best cake recipe I have ever tasted in my life. Sophia has sent it to me from the States. The lady of the house has a big book called *"The Way to a Man's Heart"*. This is a recipe from it. It tastes so good. If you ever have to bake anything for Danny, bake this one.

Family Favourite Sponge Cake

Ingredients:
- 335g / 12 oz /1.5 cups caster or granulated sugar
- 115 ml / 1/2 cup water
- 6 eggs, yolks and whites beaten separately
- 1 teaspoon vanilla essence
- 110g / 4oz /1 cup plain flour
- 1/2 teaspoon cream of tartar

Method:
1. Grease and line a 24 cm / 9.5 inch spring form cake tin. Preheat oven to 170C / 325F / Gas Mark 3.
2. Sieve the flour with the cream of tartar 4 times and set aside.
3. Whisk egg whites until stiff enough to hold up in peaks, but still shiny.
4. Put egg yolks and vanilla essence in a separate bowl and whisk well.
5. Put sugar in a saucepan with the water and boil until it threads when dropped from the end of a spoon. (be patient!)
6. Pour gradually in a fine stream on stiffly beaten whites of eggs, whisking until cool.

7. Then add the well beaten egg yolks.
8. Carefully add the sieved flour a little at a time in a fine dusting, folding in gently.
9. Transfer carefully to prepared tin and bake for about 50 minutes.

This cake is ever so soft. It slices really easily, so it's perfect for filling with whatever takes your fancy. It's bound to impress even the best baker in the world. I hope it brings you good luck Eliza!
Sophia says the Logan's entertain guests a lot and serve all sorts of dainty little sandwiches. She says these rolled sandwiches look lovely, and seem to taste nicer than ordinary sandwiches because of how they're presented.

Rolled Sandwiches

1. Use very fresh bread. Remove crusts.
2. Spread evenly with creamed butter, and over this any well seasoned and minced sandwich filling.
3. Roll each slice closely, wrap in a damp cloth, set aside until firm.
4. Cut in thin slices.

It's fun to practice making these at home, even though Father laughs at how small they are. He does admit that they seem to taste better than regular sized sandwiches.
I hope that all's okay with you and Danny in Nottingham. Please write soon, I look forward to your letters so much,

Love,
Lillie

Christmas 1911
Nottingham

Dear Lillie,

Thank you so much for sending me Sophia's sponge cake recipe. I told Danny that Sophia had sent it to you from the States and he said he'd like to have a look at it. So I wrote it out for him and he says it's one of the best sponge cake recipes he's ever seen. I was so happy to see him so pleased and then he dropped the news. He says he has acquired work in New York and he is to leave next April. It felt like my whole world had just fallen apart. Then he held me close to him and kissed me for so long it seemed like time was standing still. I feel so helpless and confused Lillie. I love him so much. I don't want it ever to be next April.
I hope you have a lovely Christmas.
                                      Love,
                                      Eliza

Friday January 5th 1912
Cavan

Dear Eliza,
        Please try and stop worrying, and don't let Danny see you too upset. Stay strong and let him see you are happy that this chance has come up for him.
Sophia's friend Bridget still tells her lots of sayings from Goethe. She says one that has made a lot of sense to her since she met her new love is this,

"To be loved for what one is, is the greatest exception. The great majority love in others only what they lend him, their own selves, their version of him."

If you could keep this in your head all the time and only wish what is best for Danny; that way he may feel how much you really love him and miss you when he's gone. Love him as he is and share his hopes and dreams Eliza. Keep your individuality at the same time and let him see that you have your own identity and character too. You'll have to be very strong and hope that what is best for you both will work out.
Aunt Minnie says Elizabeth Carmichael Ferrall's book is going to be good – the second recipe has arrived from a man! His name is Mr Edward Vicars Hamilton and he's a solicitor in Omagh, Co. Tyrone. Here it is! I was looking at this and wondering does Edwards Vicars Hamilton make this himself. I imagine he's very busy being a solicitor. Maybe he finds it relaxing making jam in his free time. Or perhaps it's an old family recipe which has been passed down to him.

I am thinking of you a lot at the moment. Keep really strong Eliza. I have my fingers crossed for you.
                Love,
                Lillie

Marrow Marmalade

By Edward Vicars Hamilton, Solicitor, Omagh

Ingredients:
- 1.7 kg / 4 lb vegetable marrow
- 900g / 2 lb apples
- 2.7 kg / 6 lb / 12 cups sugar
- juice and rind of 3 lemons
- 55g / 2 oz of whole ginger
- small teaspoonful of cayenne pepper
- 1 glass of whiskey

Method:
1. Slice the marrow, and sprinkle 450g / 1 lb / 2 cups of the sugar on it overnight.
2. Slice the apples in the same way as you would for a tart.
3. Cut the rind of the lemons as fine as possible, also the ginger, and add these with the remaining sugar to the sliced marrow.
4. Boil all slowly for 2 hours; the syrup should be thick and clear, then add the whiskey and cayenne; allow all to boil for a minute, when it will be done.

Sunday March 31st 1912
Nottingham

Dear Lillie,

    Thank you for your letter. I have done what you said and kept strong, on the outside at least, though my heart is breaking inside. Danny has left. He's gone home to Ireland to say goodbye to his mother before boarding the Titanic at Queenstown in Cork. He is to sail on her maiden voyage. The directors here have paid his fare and presented him with one of their Thomas Farrar patented "Isobel" rolling pins. There's no going back now. Lillie, I feel utterly terrible. I am trying to go on as normal but everything I look at makes me think of Danny. My heart feels like it's breaking. When he was saying goodbye he held me so long it was like he never wanted to let me go. He'll soon forget about me in New York I'm sure... but then every time I begin to think like that I try and pull myself together and remember your advice.

We've been having really strong gales here in Nottingham. They began at the start of the month. The thunderstorms seemed to echo how awful everything felt. We even had hailstones. All in all it's been a horrible month, though I've tried to do what you say and keep the bright side out. I must believe the sun will shine again and am just trying not to think about much at the moment.

I am sorry I haven't got anything cheery to say, I know I sound so miserable. Please write soon Lillie,

                Love,
                    Eliza

Thursday April 11*th* 1912
Cavan

Dear Eliza,

I'm so glad you were brave when Danny was leaving. I hope you're not too lonely. Keep your heart really strong Eliza. How are things at the factory now? If it does end up closing do you think you would come back home again?

Aunt Minnie has just got this chutney recipe which has been sent in by Mrs. Ynyr Burges who lives at Parkanaur, Castlecaulfield in County Tyrone. Her husband's family made their fortune with The East India Company.

Chutney
By Mrs. Ynyr Burges, Parkanaur

Ingredients:
- 450g / 1 lb / 2.15 cups brown sugar
- 225g / 1/2 lb onions
- 55g / 2 oz garlic
- 55g / 2 oz / 10 level teaspoons ground ginger
- 6g / 1/4 oz / 1 rounded teaspoon cayenne pepper
- 18g / 3/4 oz mustard
- 325g / 3/4 lb raisins, chopped very fine
- 1700 ml / 3 imperial pints vinegar
- 15 large sour apples
- enough salt to taste

Method:
1. Shred the onions and garlic very fine.
2. Mix the mustard, ginger and cayenne with a little of the vinegar.
3. Peel and core the apples and boil them in the remainder of the vinegar until quite soft, then leave to cool, adding salt to taste.
4. When cold blend all ingredients well together.

5. Put into wide necked bottles, cork well, and keep for some time before using.

Someone has sent in a brilliant anonymous tip for making Parsley Sauce and an anonymous recipe for kedgeree. The kedgeree one needs Harvey's sauce - it's lucky Aunt Margaret gave me the recipe for it a few years ago!

Green Sauce

The secret of making this is not to chop the parsley, but to put a large handful into cold water with a pinch of bicarbonate of soda, bring to a boil, then rub through a fine sieve before mixing with white sauce.

Kedgeree

Ingredients:
- 2 boiled, boned and flaked fish such as whiting
- 110 g / 4 oz / 1/2 cup long grain rice, soaked in water for half an hour
- 2 hard-boiled eggs, chopped
- a piece of butter the size of a large plum
- salt and pepper
- a little Harvey's sauce, according to taste

Method:
1. Drain the rice, cover with fresh water and boil until cooked.
2. Mix all ingredients together, warm in a saucepan, and serve in a warmed, covered dish.

Have you any more recipes you could send me please Eliza? It would take your mind off everything. I always loved putting the ones you used to send me into my little recipe book.

>Please write soon.
>
>Love,
>
>Lillie

Tuesday April 16ᵗʰ 1912
Nottingham

Dear Lillie,

      Have you heard the news? The Titanic has been in collision with an iceberg. Today's edition of the Daily Mirror newspaper says everyone is safe. They say many steamers rushed to help and that the ship is now on its way to to Halifax, either under its own steam, or is being towed by the Allan liner Virginian. It says they're due at Halifax in Nova Scotia today and that all the passengers will then be taken by train to New York. It says direct news was received from the Titanic last night by the parents of the wireless operator on board who wired that the boat is practically unsinkable and was slowly headed for Halifax.

How awful for Danny. I even saw Tommy's picture in the paper a few weeks ago. It said he was to represent Harland and Wolff on the Titanic's maiden voyage too. He seems to have become their main man from what I read. It would be strange if Danny and Tommy were to bump into each other and get talking. I don't think Tommy would remember the young girl he bumped into in the hallway of the house where Aunt Annie worked.

I wonder did Danny manage to save his recipes off the ship. They're so important to him; his life's work all packed into one book Lillie. And that rolling pin that Coombs gave him as he was leaving. He said that would be his good luck mascot.

Oh Lillie, he promised to write as soon as he got to New York. I hope he remembers to with all this going on. I love him with all my heart,

                                                                          Love,

                                                                          Eliza

Wednesday April 17*th* 1912
Nottingham

Dear Lillie,

The news today is worse than one could ever imagine. Yesterday's reports were false. The papers today say "only 868 alive out of 2200 on sunken liner Titanic". The very first page of the Daily Mirror has a large photograph of men embarking on the Titanic at Queenstown last Thursday. I have searched the photograph for Danny but I can't see him. The newspaper says that most of the survivors are women and children as the old chivalry code of conduct was adhered to. Ther's a list of some of the survivors' names in the paper today but they are all first and second class passengers. I believe Danny was travelling third class, though I can't be sure of that.
I must keep my head down Lillie and keep working as best I can. All I can hope for now is a miracle. I will search the paper every day for news. There weren't enough lifeboats on the ship for everyone. That was the same problem at Birkenhead 60 years ago. Why was that not a lesson to the shipbuilders for the future? I feel so sick Lillie. My tummy is in knots and I keep thinking of Danny holding me so tightly before he left. It's like he knew he would never see me again.
I wonder what about Tommy…there's no mention of him in the paper either. The American millionaire Colonel J.J. Astor's body has been picked up dead. If he didn't get a space in the lifeboats I fear there are no men left alive.

Eliza

Thursday April 18th 1912
Nottingham

Dear Mother,
            I write to you with a heavy heart. I'm sure by now you've heard the terrible news about the Titanic liner. Well Mother, for the last two years I 've been courting a lad called Danny from Mayo. He is a Master Baker and has been helping the directors in the factory here to develop new products. When they told him that the factory was getting into a little financial difficulty he made the decision to take work in The States. The awful thing is he was to board the Titanic at Queenstown. He went home to say goodbye to his mother first. Yesterday the paper said that there were 868 survivors; today it says there are only 705. I feel like my heart is breaking.
One of the headings in the paper today scared me so much Mother. It says "Irish girls fiance among the missing passengers". It says a young Irish girl came home from boarding school for Easter, and instead of going back to school like her parents thought she would, she met her sweetheart and they booked passages on the Titanic from Queenstown, as if they were brother and sister. They were planning on getting married in America. The boy did not survive, but the girl has been saved.
The paper is full of tragic stories like this one today Mother. Everyone here can talk of nothing else. The paper has listed the names of six third class passengers today who survived. Only one of them is a man. There's a photograph of passengers on board a steamer looking at broken ice floating in the North Atlantic Ocean, where the Titanic foundered. I can hardly bear to look at it. The Right Honourable A.M. Carlisle, one of the designers of the Titanic, says that he wanted to put over 40 lifeboats on the liner and commissioned enough davits for this. The board of trade only required 16 lifeboats. He says the government need to review the board of trade requirements. It is shameful that the government regulations are so inadequate.
I don't know if I'll ever hear what has happened to Danny. I don't even know his mother's address in Mayo. I want to come home Mother but as long as there's work here I will have to stay.
I love you so much Mother,
            Eliza

Narrator:
Initial newspaper reports stated that all Titanic's passengers were safe. As the full scale of the tragedy became apparent, there were many stories of coincidence and shattered dreams. Uncannily, 14 years prior to the Titanic tragedy, the American writer Morgan Robertson wrote a novella called 'The Wreck of the Titan or Futility' in 1898, published by The Quinn and Boden Co. Press. His fictitious story told of the largest ship ever built hitting an iceberg in the Atlantic ocean on a cold April night. The fictional ship named Titan and the real ship Titanic were similar in design and their circumstances were remarkably alike. Both ships were called 'unsinkable'.
Following the Titanic's sinking, some believed Robertson to be clairvoyant. Robertson denied this, claiming the similarities were explained by his extensive knowledge of shipbuilding and maritime trends. Ships were becoming larger, weren't required by law to carry sufficient lifeboats, and were travelling at speeds of over 20 knots.

Friday April 19th 1912
Nottingham

Dear Lillie,

Only an hour ago a telegram boy arrived at Coombs with this message.

"In Belfast did not board ship inform Eliza. Daniel."

Oh Lillie, I am so overcome with emotion I don't know what to believe. Could Danny really be alive? And if he is why would he be in Belfast?

I cannot find the words to write. I just had to let you know the news,

Love,

    Eliza

Friday April 19, 1912
Belfast

My dearest Eliza,
              I hope you are keeping well and everyone is doing okay at Coombs. I've something to tell you. In those last weeks before I left Nottingham I began to realise how much you really meant to me. When I held you close to say goodbye it felt like I was walking away from everything that meant anything in my life.
When I went home to say goodbye to Mam I told her all about you. She said that I must do what my heart tells me. So I did, and you've saved my life. Instead of heading south for Queenstown I headed north for your hometown. On the way here the awful news was coming through. As soon as I arrived I sent you the telegram. I'm sure you thought I was gone.
I begin work next Monday in the Bloomfield bakery in Belfast. I've found reasonable lodgings in East Bread Street, right beside the bakery. What a great address for a baker to live at! All I hope now is for you in my arms again.
Everyone here in Belfast is in a terrible state of shock about the Titanic. Even well hardened big men can't stop tears welling up in their eyes over what has happened. Many people are talking of someone called Thomas Andrews. He was Harland & Wolff's main man apparently, and by all reports was honourable to the last, trying to save as many lives as he could. They talk of him like he was their own son round here. He must have been a remarkable person.

I think I shall like living in your hometown Eliza. The people I have met in my first few hours here are so warm hearted. Please write as soon as you can,

All my love,
Danny

Sunday April 21st 1912
Belfast

Dear Eliza,
      I'm so sorrowful child dear to read your words. True love is so rare and precious and your letter brought tears to my eyes. You have so much heartache to carry Eliza.
Aunt Annie is beside herself with grief for poor Tom Andrews too. Belfast is in a state of shock Eliza.
After you left for Nottingham your Granny was so lonely for you. Over the last two winters she has found her pains getting much worse. If you saw her now you would get a terrible shock. She has slowed up a lot from those old arthritic pains in her joints.
She's barely sleeping at night and talks about you all the time. When I told her of your letter she said she wished you would come home. She says that your Great Aunt Lizzie has built up a busy trade making wedding cakes in that little hook of a kitchen of hers. Her cakes are perfect. She's so good at them sometimes she even has to turn away orders. She's killed with pains too and feels like she may have to give it up in the next year or two. Your Granny says that Aunt Lizzie is very fond of you and would teach you everything she knows. And Aunt Mary has a queue of customers at her door; she is such an accomplished tailoress. There are more than enough things you could be doing here.

I think you should come home Eliza.
                                          Love,
                                            Mother

Monday April 22nd 1912
Nottingham

Dear Mother,
        I write to let you know the most extraordinary news. Three days ago a telegram arrived at Coombs. It said this message. "In Belfast did not board ship inform Eliza. Daniel." Yesterday I received a letter from Danny saying that he couldn't bear to leave for New York and has managed to get a job in the Bloomfield Bakery in Belfast.
 I can hardly take it all in. After the shock of thinking he had perished on the Titanic, suddenly he is living and working in our hometown, just round the corner from Queen's Island. Oh how I wish I could be back home now. I hope you are all keeping well. Please tell Granny I miss her too.

                                            Love,
                                            Eliza

Monday April 22nd 1912
Nottingham

Dear Danny,

    Words cannot say how I felt to get the news. I thought you were dead Danny. I kept thinking of all your dreams and how hard you've worked all your life and I just kept crying. I've hardly slept a wink.

Do you realise how much everyone at Coombs thinks of you? When your telegram arrived it was like the best news everyone had ever received in their whole life. So many people here know of someone who perished on the Titanic. Your special mascot has brought you luck after all.

I hope that coming to Belfast will be really lucky for you too. Bloomfield Bakery is one of the best bakeries there is. Do you remember me telling you about the bread cart that calls at our house; the one that grandmother always goes out to so she can give the horse an apple? Well that's the Bloomfield Bakery breadman! Mother's favourite cake is a Florence cake which is a round plain cake with pink icing. It comes in a little greyish blue box and we all love it.

I wish I could be with you now Danny. I wish I were home in Belfast. Nottingham is such a sweet place but nowhere holds any charm for me without you.

Please write back soon and let me know how you are getting on,

All my love,

        Eliza

Thursday April 25th 1912
Belfast

Dear Eliza,
      Your letter has brought me such joy. I never let you know how much I missed you when you left for Nottingham. I didn't want to deny you the chance of a better life. When you told me all about your sweetheart I felt your pain and hurting as if it were my own. That's how a mother's heart feels Eliza.
I cannot begin to describe the emotion I felt when I read your wonderful news. What a lovely young man Danny sounds to be. You should come home Eliza. Aunt Lizzie has birthday and wedding cake orders right up until next Christmas; and that's without even thinking of finding time to make her lemon curd that everyone loves so well. She cannot continue on her own and the chance of learning her secrets and carrying on such a trade she is building up is one not to be missed. With Danny in Belfast now it's the perfect opportunity to be near him. You will both be so busy that everything will have a chance to progress slowly, and give you time to get to know each other's hearts.

Eliza, I am making up your bed tomorrow for you. Please tell me you are coming home soon,
      Love,

      Mother

Sunday April 28th 1912
Belfast

My dearest Eliza,

What a variety of bread and cake you all eat here in Belfast. I've really enjoyed my first week at the bakery. Do you know we have 100 horses and 70 bread carts? It really is a busy place.

Eliza, I would love it if you would come back to Belfast. I don't believe Coombs factory can hold out much longer. I shall keep an eye out in the local newspapers for any vacant positions which may come up.

I need to hold you again Eliza. The air of grief around here at the moment makes one want to stay close to those who really matter. I was so happy to see Mammy again; I hope you will meet her someday Eliza.

I'm adding some Ulster baker's recipes to my note-book already. The Veda bread is one I especially enjoy making.

Please write back straight away. I miss you so Eliza,

All my love,
Danny

Narrator: The Bloomfield bakery stood at the corner of the Newtownards Road between Bloomfield Avenue and East Bread Street, and was the largest bakery in Belfast. Established in 1884, and employing several hundred people, it became part of Inglis Bakeries in 1933. The premises were rebuilt in 1937 trading at the same site making cream crackers and marshmallows until 1982. Bakery Manager Tom Piggot and his two sons lost their life in the Princess Victoria sinking in 1953. In a tragedy many local people compared to the Titanic, the passenger ferry sank in one of the worst storms of the 20th century. The first Morse code message was sent out at 9.30 am, the last one at 1.58 pm. Help came too late due to other emergencies in the area at the time, and 135 people perished. The bakery premises still stand today, now housing several shops and local businesses.

Sunday 5th May 1912
Nottingham

Dear Danny,
    I 'm coming home in July. I've given in my notice and am going to help Great-Aunt Lizzie with her cake orders. Granny says she really needs help and wants someone to pass on her recipes and goodwill to, sooner or later. Did I ever tell you about all the lemon curd she makes? It's the best I have ever tasted. She told me once that her secret ingredient is a little rose water in it. Maybe she'll teach me how to make it too. Her cakes are amazing – she never seems to bother with breads or scones, just big fruit cakes that keep really well and taste amazing. When you go to her house on a visit she only ever has baker shop white bread to spread lemon curd on, and big hunks of her own wonderful fruit cake.

Oh Danny, I'm counting the days and hours till I see you again.

                                                  Love,
                                                  Eliza

Wednesday September 25th 1912
Belfast

Dear Lillie,

How lovely to be back home for autumn. The weather's been beautifully crisp and dry. Danny and I had a magical walk around Belfast last Sunday. I was skipping along through the first leaves that had fallen outside City Hall and Danny suddenly took me by the hand. The whole world seemed to stand still. I wished I could capture that moment forever.
Aunt Lizzie starts getting ready for Christmas just as the leaves change colour for autumn. The first thing she does is blend her spices. Here is her mixed spice recipe. She uses it for gingerbread, plum cakes and mincemeat.

Mixed Spice
- 14g / ½ oz / 3 level teaspoons ground allspice
- 14g / ½ oz / 3 level teaspoons ground mace
- 14g / ½ oz / 3 level teaspoons ground cinnamon
- 14g / ½ oz / 3 level teaspoons ground cloves
- 14g / ½ oz / 3 level teaspoons ground coriander
- 14g / ½ oz / 3 level teaspoons ground nutmeg

Blend all well together and store in an airtight tin.

The more time I spend with Aunt Lizzie the more I realise that she never really wants these months to come to an end. She bakes from her soul Lillie. I 'm sure that her customers can taste that in her cakes. It feels like she's passing on the essence of her heart as she chides and encourages me. The emotion is overwhelming. Sometimes when life is so bitter-sweet the whole feeling is nearly too much for one's heart to hold Lillie!

I've been looking through my old Queens College Cookbook since I got back home again. I came across a recipe called "Mysterious Pudding" that I don't remember noticing before. Here it is.

Mysterious Pudding
By Mrs. A.B. Mitchell

Ingredients:
- 2 eggs, separated
- their weight in butter, sugar, and flour
- 2 x15ml tablespoons of marmalade
- 1 rounded teaspoon baking powder

Method:
1. Beat butter to a cream; add sugar, flour, baking powder, beaten egg yolks and marmalade.
2. Beat egg whites separately until they form stiff peaks then fold into the rest of the ingredients.
3. Pour into a well-greased pudding basin.
4. Cover this with a lid or a piece of well-buttered greaseproof (waxed) paper. Cover with a double layer of kitchen foil and tie securely in place. Put the pudding in a steamer (or on an upturned plate in a saucepan) and steam gently in a pan of boiling water for about 1.5 hours (top up the water as needed to ensure the pan does not boil dry).
5. Turn the pudding out onto a warmed dish and serve immediately, accompanied by a sweet sauce.

How is everything with Sophia in Brooklyn? Is she still courting that lad from Fermanagh? I hope everything's going well for her. How is the recipe book Aunt Minnie is helping out with coming on? Please write soon,

Love,
Eliza

Wednesday November 6th 1912
Cavan

Dear Eliza,
      What a year you've been through. I'm so happy that it's all turning out so well now. We've had some surprising news from Sophia. Her sweetheart has asked her to marry him. He's also written home to his brother and asked him to look out for a small farm-holding for purchase in Fermanagh. As soon as a suitable farm is found, they're coming home!
Aunt Minnie says Elizabeth Carmichael Ferrall's recipe book is almost ready to publish. She asked Dorothy Gervais for a recipe and got quite a different type of recipe than she had expected – Dorothy Gervais lives in a big house called Cecil Manor, which isn't that far away from Augher Castle. Dorothy sent in a recipe called "Cabinet Pudding". Elizabeth says she thinks Dorothy got it out of the Women's Suffrage newspaper *"Votes for Women"* a while back, but it's going to be printed with Dorothy's name in the recipe book. Here it is Eliza –

Cabinet Pudding (comic)
Miss Dorothy Gervais, Cecil Manor, Augher, Co. Tyrone.

"Take a fresh young Suffragette, add a large idea of her own importance and as much sauce as you like, allow to stand on a Cabinet Minister's doorstep until at a white heat; mix freely with one or two policemen, well roll in the mud, and while hot run into a police court and allow to simmer; garnish with a sense of martyrdom. Popular dish, always in season. Cost, a little self-respect."

Elizabeth says there's a beautiful portrait in the Manor of Dorothy as a young girl 17 years ago. She was wearing a wonderful green cloak with a white collar at the time.

The daughter of last year's High Sheriff of Tyrone, Eleanor Story, has sent in a recipe. The family own Corick House in Clogher, which is just up the road from Augher Castle. They live in a big 15 room house in Merrion Square North in Dublin. Eleanor's father, Dr. John Benjamin Story, is a very highly regarded ophthalmic surgeon. Eleanor is 18 years old.

Savoury Rice Cutlets
By Eleanor Story, 6 Merrion Square, Dublin

1. Take a cup of cooked rice and mix with 28g / 1oz / 1/3 cup bread crumbs.
2. Add egg, some chopped parsley, grated cheese, chopped ham and seasoning to taste.
3. Spread on a buttered plate, leave to firm, then shape into cutlets.
4. Dip in whipped egg and then breadcrumbs, fry in boiling fat and serve dished in a circle.

I'm sure you're so busy with all the Christmas baking. I can't believe how quickly each year is passing. Imagine, it will soon be 1913!

Looking forward to hearing all your news soon Eliza,

Love,
Lillie

Sunday 12th January 1913
Belfast

Dear Lillie,
        Sorry I haven't replied to your letter before now. What a busy Christmas it's been. Aunt Lizzie and I could have worked day and night and still there would have been more orders for cakes. It will be very hard for her to ever give up her baking. She knows all her customers so well too. It isn't just about the cakes and the baking you know. She's afraid that if she ever gives up she would feel as if she were "done" and that's why she doesn't wish to stop and sit on her laurels, she says.

Danny's ever so busy at the bakery. I don't think anyone realises what hard work it is to be a baker. It's just as hard as working down the shipyard or in the linen industry. He's exhausted but working away, always with the thought of opening his own bakehouse in mind. He says the bread trade in Belfast is outstanding, so much so that the Industries of Ireland report says, 'There is no manufacture that we know of in the city that has shown such extraordinary advancement during recent times…It has, by the introduction of improved ferments and of ingenious machinery, been raised to a position of scientific perfection which amounts to a complete revolution.'

It's so lovely to hear that Sophia's coming home. Mother says she will find everything hard to get used to when she comes back. New York will have changed her without her even realising what's happened. Danny says that he wishes he could get his hands on the book Sophia got that sponge cake recipe you sent me out of.

Can you buy Grattan's Fruit Cordials in Cavan Lillie? Danny has fallen in love with them. He boasts about how they are the original makers and inventors of Ginger Ale; you would think he was born in Belfast the way he talks about the place now. Grattan's were established in 1825 and Granny especially enjoys their cinnamon cordial and clove cordial. Dr. Cantrell is said to have been the man who invented ginger ale along with Grattan & Company. Danny says Belfast Ginger Ale has ginger root, orange peel, nutmeg, vanilla, cinnamon and a little bit of capsicum in it. Their advertisements always have the caption "Grattan & Co., Ltd., The Original Makers

and Inventors of Ginger Ale, Belfast".
The Cabinet Pudding "recipe" was interesting. That girl Dorothy is just right to send it in to the book. Why should women work just as hard as men and get such a pitiful amount of pay? And the fines that are charged to women who are already working at slaughtering speed and fall behind a little in the linen mills is a disgrace. It's high time something were done about it for once and for all. In this day and age women are still being treated as slaves.
When I told Granny about the "suffragette recipe" she laughed. She said that if Dorothy Gervais' address is Cecil County Tyrone, she must be a descendant of Rev. Francis Gervais who built Cecil Manor in1829 and lived there until his death in 1849. He was said to have improved the lands greatly, even introducing French drains into the area. Granny says he evicted some tenants from their homes and one day received this letter:

'Death Threat to Rector "Jarvis"
Sir,
I am consciencely forced to write this letter. I mean to tell you if you evict any more of your tenants it will be recorded against you and should it be 20 years your doom will be Lord Morris. You old rascal you should be shot long ago, and I as a tenant will not pay one farthing until the suspects are released. Mind there are some good men in Tyrone that are not afraid to do away with you. Don't think this is a scam. Captain Moon-Light and Rory of the Hill are on the look-out and watch your transactions. The ball is in the gun that will "do your goose".
"Rory of the Hill".
Sacred to the memory of Gervais the old Tyrant.'

No wonder Granny goes around saying "the world's ill-divided". Father says Rector Gervais would have been Dorothy's great grandfather. Just 2 years ago Dorothy's father, Francis Peter Gervais, sold out the estate to the tenants under the Land Purchase Acts in 1911. He says Francis is a writer of books and a fine man. He wrote a book called *Shakespeare not Bacon* in 1901.
Do you know Lillie, I'll swear Danny plans to write a book someday. He's putting everything he does over at the bakery into his big book. I'm so in love with him Lillie. Please do write soon,
                                        Eliza

Monday 31ˢᵗ March 1913
Cavan

Dear Eliza,

Has the rain been bad in Belfast? It's been terrible here for the past month. Father says it's is all flooded over at Redhills because of some obstruction in the river.

Yes, we can buy Grattan's cordials in Cavan. Mam always keeps a bottle of their clove cordial in the house. It tastes really soothing and spicy.

I read your last letter over again several times. You're right about greedy landlords. Mam says landlords leech off the poor and many are no better than highway robber men. And the contempt some of them they treat their tenants with is shameful.

Imagine how different our land could be if people didn't have to slave all of their short lives just to keep a roof over their head. It's disgraceful some of the damp dwellings people are forced to pay exorbitant rents for, just because they have nowhere else to go. The more you think about it Eliza, there's something terribly evil about it all. Sophia says that since she went to the States she's thought about things differently. That old saying, "no matter how many rooms you have in your house, you can only sleep in one bed" suddenly makes sense to her now.

How's your baking with your aunt coming on? Has she taught you how to make her special lemon curd yet? Mam made this potato pudding recipe the other day. It's an old Tyrone pudding from the area where Dorothy Gervais lives. It's traditionally made at Hallowe'en, with apparently one hundred and one different ways to make it. This is how we like to make it –

Potato Pudding Recipe

Ingredients:
450g / 1 lb / about 6 medium sized mashed, cooked potatoes, still warm with 110g / 4oz/ ½ cup butter beaten into them and all put through a rice sieve

- 85g / 3oz / 1/2 cup light brown sugar
- 55g /2 oz / 1/4 cup caster sugar
- 55g / 2 oz /1/2 cup self-raising flour
- 2 beaten eggs
- pinch of salt
- one rounded teaspoon of mixed spice
- two medium eating apples
- a little warm milk to mix
- greaseproof paper, tin foil and string to cover pudding dish

Method:
1. Grease a 2 litre ovenproof glass bowl well.
2. Prepare the potatoes and butter as above, then peel, core and dice the apples.
3. Combine with the rest of the ingredients in a bowl, adding a little warmed milk if necessary, to make a thick batter.
4. Transfer pudding batter to ovenproof bowl. Cover bowl with a circle of greaseproof paper and tinfoil on top, tied well with string. Put a tray of warm water in oven. Place bowl on top and steam at 325F / 170C / Gas Mark 3 for 2 hours.

Mam says folk in County Armagh have a special recipe called "Potato Apple" which is made from potatoes and Bramley apples and is cooked on the griddle. Do you know of it Eliza?

Love,
Lillie

Wednesday 25th June 1913
Belfast

Dear Lillie,

Potato Apple's one of our favourites at home. With Granny being from County Armagh it's a bit of a speciality in our house. Granny says most every woman in the Orchard County knows the way of making potato apple. There's even a new bakery opened in Portadown last year which makes potato apple. It's run by a girl called Ruth who is helped by her sister. It's a big hit with the workingmen in the area as it reminds them of the way their mother made it.

For potato apple to work you must use Bramley cooking apples. Their unique flavour makes them an essential part of this recipe.

Potato Apple

Potato Bread Ingredients:
- 225g /8 oz / 2 medium sized potatoes
- 28g / 1 oz / 1/4 stick butter
- 85g / 3 oz / 3/4 cup plain flour

Filling:
- 140g / 5 oz /1 large Bramley cooking apple
- sugar to taste
- a knob of butter

Method:
1. Make a quantity of plain potato bread in the normal way i.e. boil potatoes and mash them while still hot. Put through a potato ricer. Add the butter and salt and then mix in the flour to form a soft dough.
2. Weigh into 2 even sized pieces. On a floured worktop, roll each piece out into a circle of about 15 cm / 6 inches in diameter.

3. Peel and core the apples and chop them into small dice. Spread the apple evenly over one circle leaving a little space around the outside. Set the second circle on top and seal around the edges with your thumbs.

4. Slide potato apple onto a lightly heated griddle. (There's no need to grease the griddle as the butter which was mashed into the potatoes is sufficient). Gently cook for about 5 minutes or until lightly browned.

5. Carefully turn over to the other side. Cut a 9cm / 3.5 inch circle out of the top of the potato apple. Sprinkle in enough sugar to sweeten. Add a little knob of butter and replace lid. Continue to cook for another 5 minutes or so, until the base is lightly browned. Serve hot, sprinkled with a little more sugar if desired.

So don't even think about making this Lillie unless you use Bramley apples. I tried making it once with ordinary windfalls and it just wasn't the same. Don't cook it too quickly or it will burn on the outside before it's nicely cooked on the inside. I hope your mam likes it and that this is the recipe she was looking for.

Last month Danny took me to the Theatre Royal in Belfast to see Joan Marvin and Thomas Rhyde in a romance of New Mexico called "Mexican Hearts Aflame". The entrance price was 3d each. Danny smoked his Golden Spangled cigarettes the whole way through the performance. He says smoking is his only relaxation. I could hardly breathe with all the smoke from so many people's cigarettes. I sat there thinking back over all that's happened since I left Belfast for Nottingham and I realised how lucky I really am. Thanks for keeping me strong when I was feeling pessimistic Lillie. I don't think I'd be here with Danny now if it hadn't been for all your advice.

That's all my news for now Lillie, looking forward to hearing from you soon,

Love,
    Eliza

Narrator: The Bank of England's online inflation calculator gives goods and services costing £1 in 1913 as costing £103.06 in 1914. There were 20 shillings in £1 and 12 pence (12d) in a shilling. That left 1d being the equivalent of around 43p in 1914, making Danny & Eliza's night out at the theatre £1.29 each in todays' money, and rather more affordable than current prices.

Sunday 29th June 1913
Nottingham

Dear Eliza,
        I hope everthing's going well for you in Belfast. Coombs are about to go into liquidation here. It's lucky that you and Daniel left when you did. I think I shall have to find employment someplace new unless someone comes along to take the factory over. It's such a shame because the products are of such high quality. There are so many customers who insist that everything turns out better when baked with Coombs Flour. I thought you would like this vol au vent of custard recipe - it's one of my favourites.

Vol au Vent of Custard

1. Make a case of puff pastry, bake it, and scoop out the inside. Place a layer of apricot preserve at the bottom.
2. Have ready custard made with an imperial pint / 568 ml of milk, a tablespoon of arrowroot, and the yolks of two eggs. Flavour with vanilla essence and a little sugar. The custard should be cooked till quite thick.
3. Pour this slowly onto the jam until level with the pastry edge. Ornament it with ratafia biscuits and chopped pistachio nuts. Bake for five minutes. Serve hot or cold.

Everyone here is in shock over the death of Emily Davison. Did you hear what happened? I haven't really got much else to tell you, but just thought I would let you know the news about Coombs,

                              Your old friend,

                                         Emily

Narrator: On 4 June 1913 suffragette Emily Davison ran in front of King George V's horse Anmer at the Epsom Derby on 4 June 1913, suffering fatal injuries, from which she died 4 days later. Pathé News captured the incident on film. A 2013 forensic examination of the old film shows that Emily may have been trying to attach a 'Votes for Women' sash to the horse rather than make herself a martyr as many historically suggested.

Tuesday 22nd July 1913
Cavan

Dear Eliza,
      I can honestly say I've never tasted anything quite like that potato apple recipe in my life. Father says it would make you go weak at the knees. It's just wonderful. Isn't the flavour of Bramley apples just gorgeous?
Eliza, Paddy has emigrated to Canada. The Labour Demand Circular of the Canadian Department of the Interior put advertisements in the paper stating that there was an urgent need for thousands of farm workers and domestic servants for Ontario and Quebec. It says that all the other provinces have similar opportunities. The Canadian government is even offering up to 160 acres of free land to settlers. All the settlers have to do is pay the land registration fee of ten dollars. They are calling Canada "The Last Best West" because there's still so much free land there. Paddy sent away for complimentary maps, pamphlets and official information from the Canadian Government Emigration Agent in Belfast. When it all arrived he could think of nothing else but leaving. His poor Mam is broken hearted. She was very brave and didn't make Paddy feel guilty over leaving. She knows he has to make his own way in the world and didn't deny him the chance at it. There are some families who try and persuade their children that emigration is a curse. I think that's a selfish kind of love. They sentence their children to a life of missed opportunities and the depression which goes hand in hand with that. It's a hard call but everyone must stand on their own two feet. Paddy has more gumption than I ever gave him credit for. I think I shall miss him Eliza!
I hope everything is going well for you with Danny. Please write soon. I love it when your letters arrive,
                Love,
                    Lillie

Monday 1ˢᵗ September 1913
Belfast

Dear Lillie,

I hope you've had a lovely summer. I told Danny about Paddy emigrating to Canada. He says Paddy's right to go. He says he's been very lucky to land such a well-paid position in Bloomfield Bakery. He's seen the wages book and knows that most men are earning less than half of what he is paid. He's worked hard and saved very carefully for the last few years. He's lucky to be one of the best paid employees in Bloomfield bakery. He has decided to buy a motor car, and one of the more reasonably priced ones available at the moment is actually one of the best looking ones I think. It's from the States. J.B. Ferguson Ltd. in Chichester Street Belfast are the sole agent for Rolls Royce, Minerva, Austin and Studebaker cars. Danny wants a 1913 model Studebaker-Flanders which is manufactured by the firm of Studebaker Brothers in Detroit. The 15-20 model is fitted out complete with an entirely new type of hood and a double screen. It costs £200. The 20-25 model is an extra £95 and has extras of a complete dynamo lighting outfit and electric self-starter. I think he will have to settle for the 15-20 model. I've seen some lovely warm pure wool fleecy motor scarves down in Anderson & McAuley's. They're £1 and 11 shillings. I wish I could buy him one.

Danny gave me one of the new English wholemeal breads which Bloomfield have the agency to bake on contract. It really does taste good. Ormeau Bakery, Megahy's, Ross's, Naylors and McWatters all have the agency to bake it. There really is such fierce competition amongst Belfast bakeries here at the minute. I think Bloomfield have an advantage as they have such a good trade built up with their outside catering business too. They're also contractors on a large scale for many Public Boards. Danny just loves working there. He says that when you use the freshest Irish eggs, best creamery butter, purest refined sugar, and the world's finest blends of milled flour, you're bound to stand head and shoulders above any of your competitors. He's so proud of the place! The Connswater River runs along just behind the bakery. Danny says it's a lovely place to sit and have a picnic lunch on its banks. The Belfast Ropeworks Company is just across the river from the bakery. It's the largest manufacturer of rope and twine in the world. Barges on the Connswater River transport raw materials to the Ropeworks and take the finished rope back to the shipyard on Queen's Island.

I'm so glad to be back in Belfast. There's something about it here that I just can't put into words. Maybe it's because it's by the waterside. Father says harbour cities built on the mouth of sandbanks have so many stories to tell. The people are earnest, but tender and friendly too. I can't really put it into words how I feel about this place. It just seems so restoring and uplifting to be back. I'm sending you a soup recipe Aunt Lizzie likes to make. It's good for when she's really busy and just wants something to eat in a hurry. She cut it out of The Northern Whig newspaper a few years ago. The clippings turned a bit yellow so it's good it will be saved in our books.

How is everything in Cavan? Please write soon and tell me all your news,
Love,
    Eliza

Red Pottage

Ingredients :
- 1/2 imperial pint / 1.2 cups haricot beans
- 1 beetroot
- 6 tomatoes (tinned or fresh)
- 1 onion
- 1 stick celery
- 1 oz butter or dripping
- 2.2 litres / 9.3 cups stock
- salt and pepper

Method:
1. Soak the beans over night, strain and rinse.
2. Scrub the beetroot, and peel it thinly; cut in slices, and put with the beans. Peel the onion, and scald it by placing it in a bowl with a pinch of salt, then covering it with boiling water, and allowing it to remain for a second or two (this is done to remove the indigestible oil which causes

3. onions to be so irritating to the eyes and also to the stomach).
4. Slice the onion, and add to the other vegetables; wash and cut celery in small pieces; cut the tomatoes in slices;
5. Next melt the butter in a saucepan, add all the vegetables, and toss in the melted butter, but on no account fry them; then add the stock and seasonings; put on the lid and simmer 4-5 hours, or until the beans are in pulp and the beetroot quite soft.
6. Puree or rub through a fine wire sieve; re-heat, and serve hot, with dice of fried bread handed separately.

Narrator: Papers were the main source of information for the public and could be purchased cheaply. Ireland had the highest literary rates in Europe and Belfast newspapers enjoyed high readership circulation figures. The Northern Whig newspaper was founded in Belfast in 1824. In 1922 the company moved to Bridge Street where they remained until 1963 when the newspaper ceased production. Along with much of nearby High Street, the building sustained sizeable damage during the Belfast Blitz in 1941. From 1963 - 1997, the building was used as office space until it was bought and turned into the Northern Whig bar and restaurant. It can be found right in the heart of Belfast's stylish Cathedral Quarter.

Wednesday 10thth December 1913
Cavan

Dear Eliza,
    Have you heard the new song "Danny Boy"? An Englishman called Frederick Weatherly has written it to the old Irish tune "The Londonderry Air". I cried when I read the words – for this little green patch of earth that's seen so much famishment and division. Then Mam reminded me of Katharine Tynan Hinkson's words set to the same old Air. She called it 'Irish Love-Song' and when I read the words I can't help but wonder if she wrote them to a woman. Eliza, wish with every part of your being, that someday it'll no longer matter in this little place what religion or creed one chooses, or chooses not to believe in, or who one chooses to fall in love with. And wish with every part of your being, for peace in our little land and all the world.

                                Love,
                                    Lillie

Irish Love-Song

Would God I were that tender apple blossom,
Floating and falling from the twisted bough,
To lie and faint within your silken bosom,
        as that does now!
Or would I were a little burnished apple
For you to pluck me, gliding by so cold.
While sun and shade your robe of lawn will dapple
        your hair's spun gold.
Yea, would to God I were among the roses
That lean to kiss you as you float between!
While on the lowest branch a bud uncloses
        to touch you. Queen!
Nay, since you will not love, would I were growing
A happy daisy, in the garden path:
That so your silver foot might press me going.
        Even unto death!

Wednesday 17th December 1913
Belfast

Dear Lillie,
    Danny has bought his new motor car. He took me out for a trip in it last Sunday. We drove over to Queens Island and then out to Helens Bay. Everywhere looked so beautiful but it was ever so cold Lillie!
I'd never heard Katharine Tynan's Irish Love-Song before. It's very beautiful. The new song "Danny Boy" made me cry too.
Have you read Rudyard Kipling's book *"Rewards and Fairies"* Lillie? It was published in 1910. My favourite poem in it is this one called "If". It's like a recipe for life, and how to ignore the doubters, liers and haters. Rudyard's mother Alice courted the poet William Allingham from Ballyshannon in County Donegal before she met Rudyard's father!
Tomorrow I'm going to Robinson and Cleaver's. Aunt Lizzie wants me to buy her some white cashmere combinations! I think I'll buy Mother stockings and I saw some Ballbriggan wool socks in the window display that Father and Sam might like. They have lovely tan button boots with Louis heels in their window too but they cost 21 shillings a pair so I won't be getting them!

Hoping you have a lovely Christmas Lillie. Looking forward to hearing from you soon,

    Love,
        Eliza

IF
By Rudyard Kipling

If you can keep your head when all about you
    Are losing theirs and blaming it on you;
If you can trust yourself when all men doubt you,
    But make allowance for their doubting too;
If you can wait and not be tired by waiting,
    Or being lied about, don't deal in lies,
Or being hated, don't give way to hating,
    And yet don't look too good, nor talk too wise;

If you can dream - and not make dreams your master;
    If you can think - and not make thoughts your aim,
If you can meet with Triumph and Disaster
    And treat those two impostors just the same;
If you can bear to hear the truth you've spoken
    Twisted by knaves to make a trap for fools,
Or watch the things you gave your life to, broken,
    And stoop and build 'em up with worn-out tools;

If you can make one heap of all your winnings
    And risk it on one turn of pitch-and-toss,
And lose, and start again at your beginnings
    And never breathe a word about your loss;
If you can force your heart and nerve and sinew
    To serve your turn long after they are gone,
And so hold on when there is nothing in you
    Except the Will which says to them: 'Hold on!'

If you can talk with crowds and keep your virtue,
    Or walk with Kings - nor lose the common touch,
If neither foes nor loving friends can hurt you,
    If all men count with you, but none too much;
If you can fill the unforgiving minute
    With sixty seconds' worth of distance run,
Yours is the Earth and everything that's in it,
    And - which is more - you'll be a Man, my son!

Cavan
Easter 1914

Dear Eliza,

    I loved the Rudyard Kipling poem you sent me. Funny you should mention William Allingham – he's one of Aunt Margaret's favourite poets. Maybe it's because she spends so much time in Bundoran and his poetry reminds her of there.

We're so happy Sophia is home again. The newly wedded lovebirds are settling in well on their little farm. You were right when you said that America would change my sister. She has her hair set in beautiful waves. She seems to walk much taller, with her shoulders back, and carries an air of confidence that seems to see right through any gloomy talk.

Mrs Logan bought Sophia her very own copy of the book '*The Way to a Man's Heart*' when she was leaving. She has brought it back in her trunk and says she's so glad she could bring a little bit of America home with her.

Peter and Sophia have come to visit Mam today. Sophia says the Irishman's son Henry Ford is making a fortune in the States. She says he has just introduced a $5 a day wage to workers in his motor car factory. That's more than double the pay they had been getting. There's been a lot of accidents in the new motor cars here in the last few months. Peter was surprised by all this talk at the moment of putting a speed limit of 8 mph in Ireland to curb the excessive velocity of the drivers.

Peter and Sophia have gone out for a walk down the road. I'm going to take a proper look now at Sophia's book before she takes it back home to Fermanagh with her. I'm so excited I can't wait to turn the pages,

                                              Love,
                                                  Lillie

Some recipes and advice from

THE WAY TO A MAN'S HEART

By Lizzie Black Kander –

The recipe book Sophia brought back from USA

SOME HOUSEHOLD RULES

How to Measure

Accurate measurement is essential to ensure good cooking.
A cupful is a 236 ml measuring cup filled LEVEL or even. To measure dry ingredients such as flour and sugar, fill lightly with a spoon, taking care not to shake the cup.

Setting the Table

The Table should be placed in the middle of the dining room, with the centre placed directly under the central light.
Silence Cloth - Cover the table with a silence cloth of felt padding or Canton flannel. Over this spread a spotless table cloth evenly, the middle crease dividing the table exactly in half.
A Cover consists of plates, glasses, silver and napkin to be used by one person. The "covers" should be directly opposite each other, allowing 25 - 30 inches / 60 - 75 centimetres from plate to plate.
Heat Dishes in which warm food is served, and chill dishes for salads and ices.
Service Plate - This plate should be placed 1 inch /2.5 cm from the edge of the table and should remain in place until the salad is served. On the service plate is placed the plate containing the cocktail glass for fruit or oysters, the appetizer, the soup plate and the hot plate for the main course.
The Knives - Sharp edges towards the plate, are placed to the right, followed by the soup spoon, bowl turned up, with the cocktail fork at the extreme right end.
The Forks - Prongs turned up, are placed to the left of the service plate.
The Spoons - Bowls turned up, handles to the right, are placed above the service plate, the after-dinner coffee spoon being nearest the plate. All silver should be placed in the order in which it is used, beginning farthest from the plate and continuing towards the plate.
The Water Glass should stand a short distance from the knife.
The Bread and Butter Plate - At the top and a bit to the left of the forks, the spreader on the plate, edge turned in and handles slanting towards the right.

The Napkin is placed to the left of the forks with the fold at the top, the hemmed edges parallel with the forks and the table edge.

Silver for the dessert course is not put on with the other silver at a formal dinner, nor are more than 3 forks laid. Additional silver is brought in with the salad or dessert, either on the plate or placed from a napkin or tray at the right of the plate.

Individual Salt and Pepper Sets are placed above each plate, or between each 2 covers.

Side Board and Serving Table are used to hold all extras which may be needed during a meal. All silver for serving should be laid out on the serving table.

A Waitress stands at the left of each person, whether she is passing a dish from which one helps himself, or placing or removing a plate.

In passing individual portions, side dishes and all drinks from which the person does not help himself - the waitress sets these down slowly and easily from the right hand side.

All used dishes should be removed from the side from which they are served. When exchanging, passing or placing a plate, the thumb should never touch the upper surface of the plate. If removing and placing, use the left hand for the plate containing food and the right hand for the empty plates.

In passing dishes from which a person helps himself, have a squarely folded large napkin or doily in the palm of the left hand under the dish, with the serving silver conveniently placed.

A tray, with a doily, is used in passing or removing sugar and cream, or salt and pepper.

Proper Dress For The Kitchen –

Jewelry should not be worn in the kitchen.

Wear a washable cap that covers the hair.

Always wear rubber gloves to protect your hands when washing up.

Do not taste from the mixing spoon; pour from the mixing spoon into a teaspoon and taste from this.

Do not taste from a spoon or drink from a glass cup that has been used by another person, without first washing it.

Do not blow on food to cool it.

Buttermilk Soda Bread

Ingredients:
- 450g / 1 lb / 4 cups flour
- ¼ teaspoon salt
- 1 teaspoon sugar
- 1 teaspoon bicarbonate of soda
- 2 teaspoons cream of tartar
- 1 egg, beaten
- 355 ml / 1.5 cups buttermilk

Method:
1. Sieve the dry ingredients, add the rest and mix well.
2. Place in a well greased and floured loaf pan and bake in a moderate oven 180C / 350F / Gas Mark 4 for 35 minutes.

Cocoa Bread

Ingredients:
- 14 g / 1/2 oz compressed fresh yeast
- 236 ml / 1 cup hot milk
- 55g / 2 oz / 1/4 cup sugar
- 2 tablespoons butter
- 1 teaspoon salt
- 1 egg, slightly beaten
- 335 g / 12 oz / 3 cups bread flour
- 28g / 1 oz / 1/4 cup cocoa

Method:
1. Place yeast with 1 teaspoon of sugar in 60 ml / 1/4 cup lukewarm water until dissolved.
2. Put butter, salt and sugar in mixing bowl.
3. Add dissolved yeast and beaten egg; beat until smooth.
4. Stir in the flour and cocoa, knead lightly to form a soft dough, (about 10

minutes by hand) adding more flour if necessary.
5. Cover and set in a warm place until double its bulk.
6. Toss on floured board, form into loaf and place in bread pan.
7. Leave to double in size again then bake at 350F / 180C / Gas Mark 4 for 45 minutes or until well done.

Peanut Butter Bread

Ingredients:
225g / 8 oz / 2 cups plain flour
4 level teaspoons baking powder
1 level teaspoon salt
55g / 2 oz / 1/4 cup caster sugar
170g / 6 oz / 2/3 cup peanut butter
295 ml / 1.25 cups milk

Method:
Sieve flour, baking powder, salt and sugar together.
Add milk to peanut butter, blend well and add to dry ingredients; beat thoroughly.
The dough must be soft enough to take the shape of the pan.
Bake in a greased loaf pan at 350F / 180C / Gas Mark 4 for 45 minutes - 50 minutes.

Parker House Rolls

Ingredients:
- 470 ml / 2 cups scalded milk
- 3 tablespoons butter + some melted butter to brush rolls with
- 2 tablespoon sugar
- 1 teaspoon salt
- 28g / 1 oz compressed fresh yeast
- 615g / 1 lb 6 oz / 5.5 cups bread flour

Method:
1. Add butter, sugar and salt to milk.
2. When melted and lukewarm, add yeast dissolved in 60 ml / 1/4 cup lukewarm water. Stir in the flour gradually and form a soft dough (about 10 minutes), adding only enough more flour to knead. Cover and let rise in a warm place until double its bulk.
3. Toss gently on floured board, handle as little as possible so as not to disturb the air bubbles.
4. Pat or roll 1/3 inch / 1 cm thick, brush well with melted butter, cut into rounds 2.5 inches/ 6 cms in diameter. Fold over double so edges meet.
5. Press finger through centre of edges to keep shape.
6. Place in rows close together in greased pans, let stand until slightly risen, then bake at 450F / 230C / Gas Mark 8 for 12 - 15 minutes, decreasing the heat over baking time.

Makes about 4 dozen rolls.

Clover Leaf Tea Rolls

Ingredients:
- 236 ml / 1 cup milk
- 170g / 6 oz / 1.5 cups bread flour + extra to make to a kneadable dough
- 1.5 teaspoons salt
- 80g / 3 oz /1/3 cup butter
- 28g / 1 oz fresh compressed yeast
- 55g / 2 oz / 1/4 cup sugar
- 2 eggs

Method:
1. Scald milk; when lukewarm, dissolve yeast in it and add 1.5 cups flour. Beat thoroughly, cover, and leave to stand until light.
2. Add sugar, salt, eggs, butter and enough more flour to knead.
3. Knead for about 10 minutes.
4. Allow to rise again until light.

5. Grease muffin pans, roll dough into 2.5 cm / 1 inch balls, place 3 in each cup, brushing melted butter between.
6. Leave to rise again, then bake at 400F / 200C /Gas Mark 6 until baked through.

French Toast

Ingredients:
- 2 eggs
- 1/2 teaspoon salt
- 155 ml / 2/3 cup milk
- 6 slices slightly stale bread
- sugar and ground cinnamon

Method:
1. Have a hot griddle or bakestone ready, butter it well.
2. Beat the egg slightly, add salt and milk, dip the bread in the mixture.
3. Brown the bread on each side on the hot griddle.
4. Serve hot sprinked with sugar and cinnamon.

Toast Points

Sliced bread toasted, then the crusts removed and cut into triangles is called Toast Points, and is used for garnishing.

Melba Toast

Cut bread as thin as possible and brown in the oven until crisp.

Sandwich Fillings

For fancy, decorated sandwiches, butter is creamed, a little lemon juice added, and run through a pastry tube with a nozzle of any design.

Cream or cottage cheese may be coloured with vegetable colouring and used as a decoration or formed into rosettes.

Suggestions for Flavoured Butters

Pimento Butter
1. Cream half a cup of butter.
2. Drain 3 large pimentos (cherry peppers) and dry.
3. Rub through a sieve (or processor) and work the pulp into the creamed butter.
4. Season with salt.

Green Pepper Butter
1. Core and deseed 3 or 4 green peppers.
2. Cook in boiling water until soft.
3. Drain well and chop fine.
4. Drain again and rub through a sieve
5. Add pulp to ½ cup creamed butter and a few grains of cayenne.

Open Faced Sandwiches

Tomato Open Faced Sandwiches –
1. With a large biscuit cutter cut sliced bread into rounds.
2. Take half of these rounds, and using a smaller biscuit cutter remove the inside of half of these to form rings.
3. Spread the large rounds with creamed butter.
4. Set some lettuce on top covered with mayonnaise, then a slice of tomato on top.
5. Season to taste and set the rings on top.

Watercress Open Faced Sandwiches

1. Pick over, wash, drain and chop about half a cup of watercress and mix with softened cream cheese.
2. Make into sandwiches in the same way as the previous tomato sandwich recipe.

Club Sandwiches

1. Butter 3 slices of hot toasted bread.
2. On one piece place sliced cold roast chicken and thin slices of fried bacon.
3. On second piece put mayonnaise, lettuce and fresh sliced tomato.
4. Cover with the third slice of bread and place on a plate.
5. Cut in half diagonally and decorate with pickles, red radishes and olives.

Sardine and Cucumber Sandwiches

Dainty little sandwiches, perfect for a picnic by the lake. Try packing the ingredients in 3 separate containers and assembling the sandwiches just before eating.

1. Take a small tin of sardines, drain off all the oil, remove skin and bone and pound the fish very finely.
2. Cut thin slices of cucumber, season with pepper and salt, and stand aside for 10 minutes.
3. With a scone or biscuit cutter, cut slices of buttered bread into rounds the size of the cucumber.
4. On each piece of bread and butter lay a piece of cucumber, with a good thick layer of the fish between. Press lightly together and serve.

Apple, Celery & Nut Salad (Waldorf)

Ingredients:
- 2 cups celery, cut
- 2 cups apples, sliced
- lettuce
- 1 cup pecan nuts and walnuts, crumbled
- mayonnaise

Method:
1. Clean the celery and lettuce and keep them crisp in the fridge.
2. When ready to serve, cut the celery in thin, crescent shaped pieces.
3. Remove the core and skin of the apple, cut in eighths and dice.
4. Crumble in the pecan nuts and walnuts.
5. Mix with mayonnaise to hold together.
6. Arrange the mixture on a platter in a mound with lettuce around the edge. Two figs cut in small pieces may be added.

Warm Potato Salad

The bits of fried bacon or beef may be omitted. If the salad is too dry add a little hot water. It should have a glassy look, without being lumpy or greasy.

Ingredients:
- 900g / 2 lb boiled potatoes sliced
- 110 g / 4 oz bacon or fat smoked beef or 2 tablespoons poultry fat
- 1 medium onion, cut fine
- 1 teaspoon salt
- ½ teaspoon sugar
- ½ teaspoon flour
- 120ml / ½ cup white vinegar
- 120 ml / ½ cup water
- 1 teaspoon mustard
- 1/8 teaspoon pepper

Method:
1. Scrub the potatoes and cook in boiling salted water until tender.
2. Drain and while hot, skin and cut into ¼ inch /1/2 cm slices.
3. Sprinkle with the salt, pepper, sugar and flour.
4. Add water to vinegar and heat thoroughly. Mix in the mustard.
5. Chop bacon or sliced beef finely. Fry until light brown.
6. Add onion and brown slightly.
7. Add potatoes and pour over the hot water and vinegar.
8. Heat all through to absorb the vinegar and water, place in a serving dish and serve warm.

Blackstone Salad Dressing

Ingredients:
- 1 cup mayonnaise
- 155 ml / 2/3 cup olive oil
- 75 ml / 1/3 cup white vinegar
- 3 tablespoons chilli sauce
- 3 pimentos, finely chopped
- 1 small grey shallot or pearl onion, finely chopped
- ¼ teaspoon salt
- pepper to taste

Method:
1. Put the mayonnaise in a bowl then add the ingredients in the order given and mix well.
2. Serve ice cold over quartered head lettuce, tomatoes, etc

Thousand Island Dressing

Serve ice cold over any salad

Ingredients:
- 2 tablespoons green peppers, cut fine
- 2 tablespoons pimento, cut fine
- 1 teaspoon onion juice or pearl onions cut fine
- 1 hard boiled egg, chopped
- 1 teaspoon Worcestershire sauce
- 1 tablespoon tomato ketchup
- 2 tablespoons chilli sauce
- 85g / 3 oz / ¾ cup whipped cream
- 250g / 9 oz / 1 cup mayonnaise
- a little salt and paprika to season

Method:
1. Mix the first 7 ingredients together.
2. Add a little salt and paprika.
3. Blend thoroughly with the mayonnaise and fold in the whipped cream.

Rinktum-Dity

Ingredients:
- 1 can tomatoes, chopped
- 110g / 4 oz / 1 cup grated cheese
- the juice of half a small grated onion
- 1 green pepper, chopped
- 2 tablespoons butter
- 2 eggs, well beaten
- 1 teaspoon salt

Method:
1. Mix chopped tomatoes, salt, cheese, onion juice and the pepper together.
2. Melt the butter, add the mixture and heat well.

3. Add the eggs and cook until the eggs are of a creamy consistency, stirring and scraping from the bottom of the pan.
4. Serve at once on toast.

Scrambled Egg Sandwich

1. Chop a few slices of bacon, some green pepper and onion very finely and fry to a light brown.
2. Into this mixture, scramble some eggs, salt and pepper to taste and serve on slices of bread or toast.

Raw Cranberry Relish

Ingredients:
- 450g / 1 lb cranberries
- 1 large orange
- 450g / 1 lb / 2 cups sugar
- 1 cup crushed pineapple (optional)

Method:
1. Put the cranberries and orange (rind and pulp) through a food chopper (processor).
2. Add sugar and mix thoroughly.
3. Let stand for several days.
4. 1 cup of crushed pineapple may be added.
5. Serve with meat.

Oysters Au Gratin

Ingredients:
- 18 oysters
- 18 mushrooms
- 2 tablespoons butter
- 1/2 teaspoon salt
- 1/8 teaspoon red pepper
- 1 cup White Sauce
- cracker crumbs and butter for topping

Method:
1. Cook the mushrooms a few minutes in hot butter.
2. Place 3 oysters on an oyster shell, then the mushroom, some white sauce, and seasoning.
3. Sprinkle with cracker crumbs and butter and bake until brown.

Fried Oysters

Ingredients:
- 24 large oysters
- 1 teaspoon salt
- 1/2 cup breadcrumbs
- 1 egg
- 1/8 teaspoon pepper

Method:
1. Clean and drain select oysters.
2. Roll in breadcrumbs, seasoned with salt and pepper.
3. Let stand 15 minutes or more, then dip in beaten egg, roll in breadcrumbs again, and leave to stand for another 15 minutes in a cool place.
4. Fry for 1 minute or until golden brown in deep, hot fat.
5. Drain on paper, serve on a hot platter and garnish with parsley, sliced pickle or lemon. Serve with French Fried Potatoes.

Oysters Manhattan Style

Ingredients:
- 24 oysters
- 24 slices bacon, to cover each oyster
- 1.5 tablespoons butter
- 1/2 teaspoon paprika
- 1/2 tablespoon salt
- 1 tablespoon parsley, finely chopped
- 2 lemons, quartered

Method:
1. Allow 3 to 6 oysters per person.
2. Have oysters freshly opened and on deep part of the shell.
3. Cream the butter, add the rest of the ingredients.
4. Divide this mixture and put a bit on each oyster.
5. Cover each oyster with a slice of bacon.
6. Set shells on a baking tin and put in a hot oven.
7. Cook for about 12 minutes, or until bacon is crisp.
8. Serve at once with a quarter of lemon.

Oysters in Blankets

Ingredients:
- 12 firm oysters
- red pepper
- 12 thin slices bacon
- chopped parsley

Method:
1. Drain oysters well and wipe dry. Lay each oyster on a thin slice of bacon.
2. Add a little red pepper, sprinkle with chopped parsley, fold bacon around oysters, fasten with a wooden cocktail stick.
3. Brown slowly in a frying pan and serve very hot.

Frog Legs hit the news in London in 1908 when the Savoy Hotel's French chef August Escoffier served them at a grand soirée in honour of the Prince of Wales. Whether they were a suitable inclusion in *The Way to a Man's Heart* cookbook or not, very much depended on the man you were cooking for.

Frog Legs

Ingredients:
- a dozen or more frog legs
- 2 tablespoons butter
- 120 ml / 1/2 cup soup stock
- salt and cayenne pepper
- 240 ml / 1 cup cream
- 3 egg yolks

Method:
1. Boil the frog legs in salt water and drain.
2. Heat 2 tablespoons butter, add 120 ml / 1/2 cup soup stock, salt and cayenne pepper to taste.
3. Boil for 3 minutes.
4. Add 240 ml / 1 cup cream and 3 egg yolks slightly beaten.
5. Cook for 2 minutes, stirring constantly and pour over the frog legs.

Frog Legs, Fried

Scald the frogs' legs for just a moment; drain and dry.
Dust with salt and pepper, dip in beaten egg; then in rolled cracker crumbs.
Let stand for 10 minutes.
Fry quickly in deep, hot fat.

O'Brien Potatoes

Ingredients:
- 1 litre container full of raw potato balls
- 2 tablespoons butter
- 2 slices of onion
- 3 canned pimentos OR 1 large green pepper, chopped
- 1 tablespoon chopped parsley

Method:

1. Peel potatoes and shape into balls with a potato baller.
2. Soak in cold water and drain well.
3. Fry in deep, hot fat until brown and tender.
4. Drain and sprinkle with salt.
5. Fry onion in 2 tablespoons butter until golden brown, remove onion, add chopped pimemtos or pepper to the butter, then the fried potatoes.
6. Serve hot sprinkled with finely chopped parsley.

Mustard for the Table

Ingredients:
1 teaspoon sugar
1/8 teaspoon salt
1 tablespoon salad oil
2 tablespoons ground mustard
2 tablespoons vinegar

Method:
Mix salt and sugar and stir in the oil thoroughly.
Add the vinegar to the ground mustard and combine the mixtures.
If too thick add a little boiling water.

Sweet Treats
Apple Strudel

Ingredients:
- 170g / 6 oz / 1.5 cups flour
- 1/4 teaspoon salt
- 80 ml / 1/3 cup warm water
- 1 egg, slightly beaten
- as many whole Bramley cooking apples or sour apples as fit into a 2 quart / 2.25 litre jug
- 170 g / 6 oz / 1 cup raisins
- 1 teaspoon ground cinnamon
- 85g / 3 oz / 1/2 cup currants
- 110g / 4 oz / 1/2 cup butter, melted
- 110g / 4 oz almonds, chopped and blanched
- 225g / 8 oz / 1 cup sugar
- 55g / 2 oz / 1/2 cup digestive biscuit / Graham cracker crumbs/ sponge cake crumbs or breadcrumbs

Method:
1. Put the salt, flour and egg into a large mixing bowl.
2. Add the warm water and mix the dough quickly with a knife.
3. Turn out onto a floured worktop and knead, stretching it up and down to make it elastic, until it leaves the board clean.
4. Toss it onto a well-floured bread board, cover with a hot bowl and leave in a warm place for half an hour or longer, so that it will stretch easily.
5. Lay the dough in the centre of a well-floured smooth extra large cotton tea towel or cotton pillowcase on a large table.
6. Brush well with some of the melted butter.
7. Put your hands under the dough palms down, and pull and stretch the dough gently, and then gradually around the edges until it is almost as large as the cloth and thin as paper.
8. Peel and core the apples and chop up finely.

9. Sprinkle apples, raisins, currants, almonds, sugar and cinnamon evenly over ¾ of the dough.
10. Finely sprinkle the digestive biscuit / Graham cracker crumbs evenly over the fruit and nut mixture.
11. Drip a few tablespoons of the melted butter evenly over all of this.
12. Trim the edges.
13. Fold the dough over apples on one side, then hold cloth high with both hands and the strudel will roll itself over and over into a big roll.
14. Trim the edges again.
15. Now twist the roll to fit a greased pan or alternatively cut the roll into 2 or 3 strips. Brush over with melted butter.
16. Bake for 20 minutes to 1/2 hour in a hot oven 200 C / 400 F/ Gas Mark 6, then reduce heat to 180 C / 350 F / Gas Mark 4, and bake until brown and crisp.

Serve slightly warm.

Custard Sauce

Ingredients:
- 475 ml /2 cups milk, scalded
- 4 tablespoons sugar
- 1 tablespoon cornflour / cornstarch
- 1/4 teaspoon salt
- 1 teaspoon vanilla essence
- 1 egg or 2 yolks

Method:
1. Mix sugar, cornstarch and salt; add egg slightly beaten.
2. Add scalded milk, stirring constantly.
3. Cook in double boiler until it thickens and coats the spoon.
4. Sieve, cool and flavour with vanilla essence.

American Fruit or Wedding Cake

Ingredients:
- 450g / 1 lb /2 cups brown sugar
- 450g / 1 lb / 2 cups butter
- 450g / 1 lb / 4 cups flour
- 12 eggs, beaten separately
- 1 teaspoon bicarbonate of soda
- 1 teaspoon freshly grated nutmeg
- 110g / 1/4 lb each of candied orange, lemon rind and citron, cut very fine
- 140g / 5 oz / 1/2 cup molasses
- 2 teaspoons ground cinnamon
- 1 teaspoon ground cloves
- 225g / 1/2 lb blanched almonds
- 225g / 1/2 lb pecan nuts, unbroken
- 900g / 2 lbs raisins
- 450g / 1 lb sultanas
- 450g / 1 lb dates
- 450g / 1 lb figs
- 450g / 1 lb candied pineapple rings
- 450g / 1 lb candied cherries
- 118 ml / ½ cup fruit juice or wine substitute

Method:
1. Line 4 bread pans with silicone paper.
2. Preheat the oven to 150C / 300F / Gas Mark 2.
3. Cut each ring of pineapple into slices, then in half crossways.
4. Stone and cut the dates and remove the stem end from the figs.
5. Mix the dates with one cup of the flour.
6. Mix the rest of the flour with the bicarbonate of soda and spices.
7. Cream the butter and sugar well. Add the well beaten egg yolks and stir well.
8. Add the flour mixture alternately with the liquids.
9. Gently fold in the beaten egg whites, then the dates and gradually add the raisins.
10. Fill the tins in the following manner, ensuring that they're not more than

two thirds full.
Put a layer of batter in each tin, add a layer of pineapple down the centre, and fill in the spaces and sides lightly with citron, orange, lemon, cherries and nuts.
Add another layer of batter, then a layer of figs, the rest of the fruit and nuts and top with the remaining batter.
11. Fill a large pan with 1 inch / 2.5 cm of hot water. Set the pans in this the oven and bake for half an hour.
12. Next cover the pans with silicone paper and bake for 2 more hours.
13. Remove pans from the water and bake for a further half-hour reducing oven temperature a little.

Alternatively bake in a very slow oven for 4 - 5 hours at 110 C / 225 F / Gas Mark ¼.

When cool, remove from paper. Wrap in fresh waxed paper and store in a tightly covered tin box.

Stuffed Dates

Make a cut the entire length of the dates and remove stones. Fill cavities with walnuts, blanched almonds, pecans or with a mixture of chopped nuts, and reshape in original form.
Roll in granulated sugar or powdered sugar and serve on a small plate or bonbon dish.

Drinks

General Rules For Soft Drinks
Drinks must be served either very hot or very cold.
In preparing cold drinks use ice cold still, sparkling or soda water.

Chocolate Syrup

Ingredients:
- 1 quart / 1.1 litres water
- 450g / 1 lb / 2 cups sugar
- 2 tablespoons cornflour / cornstarch
- 2 teaspoons vanilla essence
- 110g /4 oz chocolate
- A good pinch of salt

Method:
1. Boil sugar and water to a syrup for 5 minutes.
2. Dissolve the cornstarch in a little cold water and add along with the chocolate and salt.
3. Stir until smooth and cook for 3 minutes.
4. Cool, add vanilla, and place in a jar in the fridge.
Use 2 tablespoons to a glass, adding milk or milk and water mixed when ready to serve.
Serve with a tablespoon of sweetened whipped cream or ice cream on top of each glass.

Pineapple Punch

Ingredients:
- 1.1 litre cold water
- 450g / 1 lb /2 cups sugar
- 118 ml /1/2 cup lemon juice
- 2 x 236 ml cups of chopped pineapple
- 236 ml /1 cup orange juice

Method:
1. Boil water, sugar and pineapple for 20 minutes.
2. Add fruit juices and allow to cool. Sieve, and dilute with iced water as required.

Dandelion Punch

Ingredients:
- 2.2 litre jug full of dandelion blossoms
- 4.4 litres boiling water
- 1350g / 3 lb sugar
- 2 oranges
- 1 lemon

Method:
1. Pour the boiling water over the dandelion blossoms and let stand overnight.
2. Slice the oranges and lemons thinly.
3. Strain dandelion water, add sugar and bring to boiling point.
4. Pour liquid over the oranges and lemons, cover and leave for 3 days.
5. Strain before serving.

Blackberry or Elderberry Cordial

Ingredients:
- 4 x 2 litre jugs full of ripe blackberries or elderberries
- 1900 ml /8 cups cold water
- 1800g / 4 lbs sugar (approximately)
- 1 tablespoon each of whole allspice, cloves and cinnamon bark
- plenty of vanilla extract

Method:
1. Tie the spices in a muslin bag.

2. Pick over and wash the berries.
3. Place in a preserving pan, cover with the water and let boil thoroughly until soft.
4. Strain well.
5. Measure juice and to every 950 mls of juice allow 450g / 2 cups of sugar and 4 tablespoons of vanilla extract (setting aside the vanilla extract until after boiling).
6. Add the spice bag to the juice and sugar and boil for about 20 minutes or until well flavoured.
7. Remove scum and stir in the vanilla extract.
8. Pour into hot sterilised jars and bottles and seal.

Tea Punch

Ingredients:
- 1 tablespoon tea leaves
- 475 ml / 2 cups boiling water
- 450g / 2 cups sugar
- juice of one lemon
- juice of one orange
- 950 mls / 4 cups sparkling water, chilled
- crushed mint leaves (optional)

Method:
1. Place tea leaves in a large earthenware pitcher and pour on boiling water.
2. Cover well with a heavy folded napkin and leave to stand for 5 minutes.
3. Add sugar and the fruit juices, and crushed mint leaves if desired.
4. Cool, and when ready to serve, add ice and the chilled soda water.

Sunshine Punch

Ingredients:
- 6 oranges
- 6 lemons
- 450g / 1 lb sugar
- 236 ml / 1 cup water
- 1 litre / 4 cups ginger ale
- 1 litre / 4 cups sparkling water

Method:
1. Boil sugar and water to syrup stage and cool.
2. Add orange and lemon juice.
3. Place in punch bowl over a cake of ice, add ginger ale and sparkling water and serve at once.

Ice Cubes

Fill ice cubes tray with water or other liquid such as ginger ale or root beer for variety.

To Decorate - colour with vegetable colouring or place a maraschino cherry, candied cherry or cranberry, or any other decoration in each compartment. When frozen, serve in lemonade or any other fruit drink.

Frozen Fruit Cubes

1. Take any type of canned fruit, mixed or of a single type and cut up fine.
2. If very sweet, add water to the juice.
3. Put fruit in ice cube compartments, cover it with juice, and let stand in freezer until frozen.
4. Serve with whipped cream, or in a salad.

Friday 25th April 2014
Belfast

Dear Friend,

      Here's the 'Pudding Recipe' Lillie promised to send. Isn't it funny how little human nature has changed since this was written in the 1830s? Some of the language chosen has slipped out of use, so I took the liberty of translating it into 21st century World English, out of the Anglo-Irish / Hiberno-English and local dialect which William Carleton captured so well. It would have been arduous for a present-day local person to read, and well nigh impossible for millions of global English speakers to engage with, or catch the gist of what Carleton was saying at the time. Pardon me if the words are a little discourteous here and there - I hope I've translated as Carleton intended, and kept as close to his pen as possible. The genre is one of farce, but with a lesson which is just as pertinent now as it was nearly 200 years ago. I trust that William Carleton would be satisfied with my transcription of 'The Pudding Bewitched', were he here with us now. I wonder how his pen would challenge the extremism and intolerance that still hates, bullys and threatens our world today under the guise of religious affiliation? I think he'd still be prescribing a little piece of party pudding, to make us forget the hate and enjoy sharing our food at the banquet table of life,

                                              With Love,
                                                    Viola

The Pudding Bewitched

"Moll Roe Rafferty was the son - daughter I meant to say - of old Jack Rafferty, who was remarkable for a habit he had of always wearing his head under his hat. Sure indeed that family was a very strange one, as everybody knew that was acquainted with them. It was said of them - but whether it was true or not I wouldn't like to take it upon myself to say, in case I'd tell a lie - that whenever they didn't wear shoes or boots they always went barefooted; but I heard afterwards that this was disputed, so rather than say anything to injure their character, I'll let that pass. Now, old Jack Rafferty had two sons, Paddy and Molly - Hey! what are you all laughing at? - I meant to say a son and daughter, and it was generally believed among the neighbours that they were brother and sister, which you know might be true or it might not: but that's a thing that, with the help of goodness, we better not discuss today.

The truth is that there were many ugly things which I wouldn't like to repeat rumoured about the family:- such as that neither Jack nor his son Paddy ever walked a perch without puttin' one foot in front of the other like a salmon.

"Moll Roe was a fine young bouncing girl, large and lavish, with a pretty head of hair on her like scarlet, that being one of the reasons why she was called Roe, or red; her arms and cheeks were much the same colour as her hair, and her saddle nose was the prettiest thing of its kind that ever was on a face. Her fists - for, thank goodness, she was blessed with a fine pair of them - had a strong similarity to two thumping turnips, reddened by the sun; and to keep all right and tight, she had a temper as fiery as her head - for, indeed, it was well known that all the Raffertys were warm-hearted. How and ever, it appears that God gives nothing in vain and of course those same fists, big and red as they were, if all that is said about them is true, were not so much given to her for ornament as for use. Combined with her lively temper, we have it upon good authority, that there was no danger of them getting blue-moulded for want of practice. She had a twist, too, in one of her eyes that was very becoming to her, and made her poor husband, when she got him, take it into his head that she could see round a corner. She caught him out in many crazy things, without doubt; but whether it was thanks to that twist in her eye or not, I wouldn't take it upon myself to say, in case I'd tell a lie.

It happened that there was a neat drifter in the neighbourhood, just as gorgeous as herself, and he was named Gusty Gillespie. Gusty, the Lord guard us, was a Presbyterian, and a complete miser with his money. Gusty was rather good-looking when seen in the dark, as was Moll herself; and, indeed, it was pretty well known that it was during nightly rendez-vous meetings that they'd really got to know each other well. The consequence of that was, that in due time both families began to talk very seriously as to what was to be done. Moll's brother, Pawdien O'Rafferty, gave Gusty the best of two choices. What they were it's not worth speaking about; but at any rate one of them was a testing question, and as Gusty knew his man, he soon came to his senses. Accordingly everything was deranged (Carleton cheekily played on the word 'arranged' here) for their marriage, and it was appointed that they should be hooked up by the Rev. Samuel M'Shuttle, the Presbyterian parson, on the following Sunday.

Now this was the first marriage that had happened for a long time in the neighbourhood between a Presbyterian and a Catholic, and of course there were strong objections on both sides against it; and my goodness, only for one thing, it would never have taken place at all. At any rate, one of the bride's uncles, old Harry Connolly, a fairy-man, who could cure all complaints with a secret he had, and as he didn't wish to see his niece married to such a fellow, he fought bitterly against the match. All Moll's friends, however, stood up for the marriage except for him, and of course the Sunday was appointed, as I said, that they were to be dove-tailed together.

Well, the day arrived, and Moll, as became her, went to Mass, and Gusty to the Presbyterian service, after which they were to join one another in Jack Rafferty's, where the priest, Father M'Sorley, was to slip up after Mass to take his dinner with them, and to keep Misther M'Shuttle, who was to marry them, company. Nobody remained at home but old Jack Rafferty and his wife, who stayed to organise the dinner, for, to tell the truth, it was to be a great spread altogether. Maybe, if all was known, too, that Father M'Sorley was to give them a blessing over and above the minister, because Moll's friends weren't altogether satisfied at the kind of marriage which M'Shuttle could give them. What odds about that anyway, all I can say is, that when Mrs. Rafferty was going to tie up a big bag pudding she was making, in walks Harry Connolly, the fairy-man, in a rage, and shouts out, - 'Blood and blunderbushes, what are you two here for?'

' What are you on about Harry? Why do you ask?'

'Why, the sun's in turmoil and the moons in the Horrocks lunar crater; there's an eclipse coming and, and there you're both as unconcerned as if it was about to rain liquor. Go out and cross yourselves three times in the name of the four Mandromarvins, for as prophecy says:- Fill the pot, Eddy, supernaculum - a blazing star's a rare spectaculum. Go out both of you and look at the sun, I say, and you'll see the condition he's in - off!'

Sure enough, Jack gave a bounce to the door, and his wife leaped like a two-year-old, and they were both stood on a stile beside the house to see what was wrong in the sky.

'Goodness, what is it, Jack,' said she; 'can you see anything?'

'No,' says he, 'with the full of my eye I can spy, nothing, except for the sun himself, that's not visible in regard of the clouds. God guard us! I doubt there's something to happen.'

'If there wasn't, Jack, what would put Harry, that knows so much, in the state he's in?'

'I doubt it's this marriage,' said Jack: 'between ourselves, it's not over and above religious for Moll to marry a Presbyterian, and only for - ; but it can't be helped now, though as you can see not a taste of the sun is willing to show his face upon it.'

'As to that,' says the wife, winking with both her eyes, 'if Gusty's satisfied with Moll, it's enough. I know who'll carry the whip hand, anyhow; but in the meantime let us ask Harry within what ails the sun.'

Well, they accordingly went in and put the question to him:
'Harry, what's wrong? What is it now, for if anybody alive knows, you do?'

'Ah!' said Harry, screwing his mouth with a kind of a dry smile, 'the sun has a hard twist of the cholic; but never mind that, I tell you you'll have a merrier wedding than you think, that's all;' and having said this, he put on his hat and left the house.

Now, Harry's answer relieved them very much, and so, after calling to him to be back for the dinner, Jack sat down to take a draw of his pipe, and the wife lost no time in tying up the pudding in a cloth and putting it in the pot to be boiled.

In this way things went on well enough for a while, Jack smoking away, and the wife cooking and dressing the food at the rate of a hunt. At last, Jack, while sitting as I said, contentedly at the fire, thought he could perceive an odd dancing kind of motion in the pot that puzzled him a good deal.

'Katty,' said he, 'what the dickens is in this pot on the fire?'

'Not a thing but the big pudding. Why do you ask?' says she.

'Why,' said he, 'if ever a pot took it into its head to dance a jig, and this did. Thunder and marbles, look at it!'

My goodness, it was true enough; there was the pot bobbing up and down and from side to side, jigging it away as merry as a little person; and it was quite easy to see that it wasn't the pot itself, but what was inside of it, that brought about the hornpipe.

'By the hole of my coat,' shouted Jack, 'there's something alive in it, or it would never cut such a dance!'

'My goodness, there is, Jack; something strange entirely has got into it. Man alive, what's to be done?'

Just as she spoke, the pot seemed to cut the buckle in prime style, and after a spring that would shame a dancing-master, off flew the lid, and out bounced the pudding itself, hopping, as nimble as a pea on a drum-head, about the floor. Jack blessed himself, and Katty crossed herself. Jack shouted, and Katty screamed. 'In the name of goodness, keep your distance; no one here injured you!'

The pudding, however, made a lunge at him, and Jack leaped first on a chair and then on the kitchen table to avoid it. It then danced towards Kitty, who was now repeating her prayers at the top of her voice, while the cunning thief of a pudding was hopping and jigging it round her, as if it was amused at her distress.

'If I could get the pitchfork,' said Jack, 'I'd deal with it - by goxty I'd try its mettle.'

'No, no,' shouted Katty, thinking there was a fairy in it; 'let us speak to it fair. Who knows what harm it might do? Easy now,' said she to the pudding, easy, dear; don't harm honest people that never meant to offend you. It wasn't us - no, in truth, it was old Harry Connolly that bewitched you; pursue him if you wish, but spare a woman like me; for, whisper, dear, I'm not in a condition to be frightened - truth I'm not.'

The pudding seemed to take her at her word, and danced away from her towards Jack, who, like the wife, believing there was a fairy in it, and that speaking fair to it was the best plan, thought he would give it a soft word as well as her.

'Please your honour,' said Jack, 'she only speaks the truth; and upon my appetite, we both feel much obliged to your honour for your quietness. Faith, it's quite clear that if you weren't a gentlemanly pudding all out, you'd act otherwise. Old Harry, the rogue, is your mark; he's just gone down the road there, and if you go fast you'll overtake him. By my song, your dancing master did his duty, anyhow. Thank your honour! God speed you, and may you never meet with a parson or high constable in your travels!'

Just as Jack spoke the pudding appeared to take the hint, for it quietly hopped out, and as the house was directly on the road-side, turned down towards the bridge, the very way that old Harry went. It was very natural, of course, that Jack and Katty should go out to see how it intended to travel; and, as the day was Sunday, it was but natural, too, that a greater number of people than usual were passing the road. This was a fact; and when Jack and his wife were seen following the pudding, the whole neighbourhood was soon up and after it.

'Jack Rafferty, what is it? Katty, ah, will you tell us what it means?'

'Why,' replied Katty, 'it's my big pudding that's bewitched, and it's now hot foot pursuing - ;' here she stopped, not wishing to mention her brother's name - 'some one or other that surely put pishrogues in it.' (put it under fairy influence.)

This was enough; Jack, now seeing that he had assistance, found his courage coming back to him; so says he to Katty, 'Go home,' says he, 'and lose no time in making another pudding as good, and here's Paddy Scanlan's wife, Bridget, says she'll let you boil it on her fire, as you'll want our own to dress the rest of the dinner: and Paddy himself will lend me a pitchfork, for chasing to the morsel of that same pudding. I'll let the wind out of it, now that I've the neighbours to back and support me,' says Jack.

This was agreed to, and Katty went back to prepare a fresh pudding, while Jack and half the townland pursued the other with spades, forks, pitchforks, scythes, flails, and all possible description of instruments. On the pudding went, however, at the rate of about six Irish miles an hour, and such a chase never was seen. Catholics, Protestants, and Presbyterians, were all after it, armed, as I said, and bad end to the thing but its own activity could save it. Here it made a hop, and there a prod was made at it; but off it went, and some-one, as eager to get a slice at it on the other side, got the prod instead of the pudding. Big Frank Farrell, the miller of Ballyboulteen, got a prod backwards that brought a hullabaloo out of him you might hear at the other end of the parish. One got a slice of a scythe, another a whack of a flail, a third a rap of a spade that made him look nine ways at once.

'Where is it going?' asked one. 'My life for you, it's on it's way to Prayers. Three cheers for it if it turns to Carnteel.' 'Prod the soul out of it, if it's a Protestant',' shouted the others; 'if it turns to the left, slice it into pancakes. We'll have no Protestant puddings here.'

My goodness, by this time the people were on the point of beginning to have a regular fight about it, when, very fortunately, it took a short turn down a little by-lane that led towards the Methodist preaching-house, and in an instant all parties were in an uproar against it as a Methodist pudding. 'It's a Wesleyan,' shouted several voices; 'and by this and by that, into a Methodist chapel it won't put a foot to-day, or we'll lose a fall. Let the wind out of it. Come, boys, where's your pitchforks?'

The devil if one of them pursuing, however, could ever touch the pudding, and just when they thought they had it up against the gavel of the Methodist chapel, didn't it gave them the slip, and hops over to the left, clean into the river, and sails away before all their eyes as light as an egg-shell.

Now, it so happened that a little below this place, the demesne-wall of Colonel Bragshaw was built up to the very edge of the river on each side of its banks; and so finding there was a stop put to their pursuit of it, they went home again, every man, woman, and child of them, puzzled to think what the pudding was at all, what it meant, or where it was going! Had Jack Rafferty and his wife been willing to let out the opinion they held about Harry Connolly bewitching it, there is no doubt of it but poor Harry might be badly treated by the crowd, when their blood was up. They had sense enough, how-and-ever, to keep that to themselves, for Harry being an old bachelor, was a kind friend to the Raffertys. So, of course, there was all kinds of talk about it - some guessing this, and some guessing that - one party saying the pudding was of their religion, another party denying it, and insisting it belonged to them, and so on.

In the meantime, Katty Rafferty, for fear dinner might come short, went home and made another pudding much about the same size as the one that had escaped, and bringing it over to their next neighbour, Paddy Scanlan's, it was put into a pot and placed on the fire to boil, hoping that it might be done in time, especially as they were to have the minister, who loved a warm slice of a good pudding as well as any a gentleman in Europe.

Anyhow, the day passed; Moll and Gusty were made man and wife, and no two could be more loving. Their friends that had been asked to the wedding were sauntering about in pleasant little groups till dinner-time, chatting and laughing; but, above all things, striving to account for the antics of the pudding; for, to tell the truth, its adventures had now gone through the whole parish.

Well, at any rate, dinner-time was drawing near, and Paddy Scanlan was sitting comfortably with his wife at the fire, the pudding boiling before their eyes, when in walks Harry Connolly, in a flutter, shouting- 'Blood an' blunderbushes, what are you two here for?'

' What are you on about Harry? Why do you ask?' said Mrs. Scanlan.
'Why, the sun's in turmoil and the moons in the Horrocks lunar crater; there's an eclipse coming and, and there you're both as unconcerned as if it was about to rain liquor. Go out both of you, an' look at the sun, I say, and you'll see the condition he's in—off!'

'Ay, but, Harry, what's that rolled up in the tail of your cothamore (big coat)?'

'Out with you both' said Harry, 'and pray aginst the eclipse —the sky's fallin'!'

Goodness, it was hard to say whether Paddy or the wife got out first, they were so much alarmed by Harry's wild thin face and piercing eyes; so out they went to see what was wonderful in the sky, and kept looking and looking in every direction, but not a thing was to be seen, except for the sun shining down with great good-humour, and not a single cloud in the sky. Paddy and the wife now came in laughing, to scold Harry, who, no doubt, was a great wag in his way when he wished. 'Well, bad scran (luck) to you,

Harry ---.' They had time to say no more, how-and-ever, for, as they were going into the door, they met him coming out of it with a reek of smoke out of his tail like a lime-kiln.

'Harry,' shouted Bridget, 'my soul to glory, but the tail of your cothamore's a-fire - you'll be burned. Don't you see the smoke that's out of it?'

'Cross yourselves three times,' said Harry, without stopping, or even looking behind him, 'for, as the prophecy says - Fill the pot, Eddy - ' They could hear no more, for Harry appeared to feel like a man that carried something a great deal hotter than he wished, as anyone might see by the liveliness of his motions, and the wild faces he was forced to make as he went along.

'What the dickens is he carrying in the skirts of his big coat?' asked Paddy.

'My soul to happiness, but maybe he has stole the pudding,' said Bridget, 'for it's known that many a strange thing he does.'

They immediately examined the pot, but found that the pudding was there as safe as tuppence, and this puzzled them the more, to think what it was he could be carrying about with him in the manner he did. But little they knew what he had done while they were sky-gazing!

Well, anyhow, the day passed and the dinner was ready, and no doubt but a fine gathering there was to partake of it. The Presbyterian minister met the Methodist preacher - a devilish stretcher of an appetite he had, in truth - on their way to Jack Rafferty's, and as he knew he could take the liberty, why he insisted on his dining with him; for, after all, my goodness, in them times the clergy of all descriptions lived upon the best footing among one another, not all as one as now - but no matter. Well, they had nearly finished their dinner, when Jack Rafferty himself asked Katty for the pudding; but, just as he spoke, in it came as big as a mess-pot.

'Gentlemen,' said he, 'I hope none of you will refuse tasting a bit of Katty's pudding; I don't mean the dancing one that took to its travels to-day, but a good solid fellow that she made since.'

'To be sure we won't,' replied the priest; 'so, Jack, put a trifle on them three plates at your right hand, and send them over here to the clergy, and maybe,' he said, laughing for he was a droll good-humoured man - 'maybe, Jack, we won't set you a proper example.'

'With a heart and a half, your reverence and gentlemen; in truth, it's not a bad example ever any of you set us at the likes, or ever will set us, I'll go bail. An' sure I only wish it was better fare I had for you; but we're humble people, gentlemen, and so you can't expect to meet here what you would in higher places.'

'Better a meal of herbs,' said the Methodist praicher, 'where peace is - .' He had time to go no farther, however; for much to his amazement, the priest and the minister started up from the table just as he was going to swallow the first spoonful of the pudding, and before you could say Jack Robinson, started away at a lively jig down the floor.

At this moment a neighbour's son came running in, an' told them that the parson was coming to see the new-married couple, and wish them all happiness; and the words were scarcely out of his mouth when he made his appearance. What to think he knew not, when he saw the minister footing it away at the rate of a wedding. He had very little time, however, to think; for, before he could sit down, up starts the Methodist preacher, and clapping his two fists in his sides, chimes in in great style along with him.

'Jack Rafferty,' says he - and, by the way, Jack was his tenant - 'what the dickens does all this mean?' says he; 'I'm amazed!'

'Not a particle of me can tell you,' says Jack; 'but will your reverence just taste a morsel of pudding, merely that the young couple may boast that you ate at their wedding; for sure if you wouldn't, who would?'

'Well,' says he, 'to gratify them I will; so just a morsel. But, Jack, this beats Bannagher,' says he again, putting the spoonful of pudding into his mouth; 'has there been drink here?'

'Oh, the devil a spud,' says Jack, 'for although there's plenty in the house, faith, it appears the gentlemen wouldn't wait for it. Unless they took it elsewhere, I can make nothing of this.'

He had scarcely spoken, when the parson, who was an active man, cut a caper a yard high, and before you could bless yourself, the three clergy were hard at work dancing, as if for a wager. My goodness, it would be unpossible for me to tell you the state the whole meeting was in when they seen this. Some were hoarse with laughing; some turned up their eyes with wonder; many thought them mad, and others thought they had turned up their little fingers a trifle too often.

'By goxty, it's a burning shame,' said one, 'to see three ribald clergy in such a state at this early hour!' 'Thunder and ounces, what's came over them at all?' says others; 'why, one would think they're bewitched. Holy Moses, look at the caper the Methodist cuts! And as for the Rector, who would think he could handle his feet at such a rate! By this and by that, he cuts the buckle, and does the triple step equal to Paddy Horaghan, the dancing-master himself? And see! Bad cess to the morsel of the parson that's not hard at Peace upon a party, an' it of a Sunday too! Whirroo, gentlemen, the fun's in you all after all - whish! more power to you all!'

The sorrow's own fun they had, and no wonder; but imagine what they felt, when all at once they saw old Jack Rafferty himself bouncing in among them, and footing it away like the best of them. My goodness, no play could match it, and nothing could be heard but laughing, shouts of encouragement, and clapping of hands like mad.

Now the minute Jack Rafferty left the chair where he had been carving the pudding, old Harry Connolly comes over and sits himself down in his place, in order to send it round, of course; and he was scarcely seated, when who should make his appearance but Barney Hartigan, the piper. Barney, by the way, had been sent for early in the day, but being away from home when the message for him went, he couldn't come any sooner.

'Begorra,' said Barney, 'you're early at the work, gentlemen! but what does this mean? But, devil may care, you won't want the music while there's a blast in the pipes, anyhow!' So saying, he gave them 'Jig Polthogue', and after that 'Kiss my Lady', in his best style.

In the meantime the fun went on thick and threefold, for it must be remembered that Harry, the old knave, was at the pudding; and maybe he didn't serve it about in double quick time too. The first he helped was the bride, and, before you could say chopstick, she was at it hard and fast before the Methodist preacher, who gave a jolly spring before her that threw them into convulsions. Harry liked this, and made up his mind soon to find partners for the rest; so he accordingly sent the pudding about like lightning; and to make a long story short, with the exception of the piper and himself, there wasn't a pair of heels in the house but were as busy at the dancing as if their lives depended on it.

'Barney,' says Harry, 'just taste a morsel of this pudding; devil the such a bully of a pudding ever you ate; here, your soul! try a snig of it - it's beautiful.'

'To be sure I will,' says Barney. 'I'm not the boy to refuse a good thing; but, Harry, be quick, for you know my hands is engaged, and it would be a thousand pities not to keep them in music, and they so well inclined. Thank you, Harry; my goodness that is a famous pudding; but blood and turnips, what's this for?'

The word was scarcely out of his mouth when he bounced up, pipes and all, and dashed into the middle of the party. 'Hurray, your souls, let us make a night of it! The Ballyboulteen boys for ever! Go for it, your reverence - turn your partner - heel and toe, minister. Good! Well done again - Whish! Hurroo! Here's for Ballyboulteen, and the sky over it!'

Bad luck to such a set that ever was seen together in this world, or will again, I suppose. The worst, however, wasn't come yet, for just as they were in the very heat and fury of the dance, what do you think comes hopping in among them but another pudding, as nimble and merry as the first! That was enough; they all had heard of—the ministers among the rest - and most of them had seen the other pudding, and knew that there must be a fairy in it, sure enough. Well, as I said, in it comes into the midst of them; but the very appearance of it was enough. Off the three clergy danced, and off the whole weddingers danced after them, every one making the best of their way home; but not one of them able to break out of the step, if they were to be hanged for it. Truth it wouldn't leave a laugh in you to see the parson dancin' down the road on his way home, and the minister and Methodist preacher cutting the buckle as they went along in the opposite direction. To make short work of it, they all danced home at last, with scarce a puff of wind in them; the bride and bridegroom danced away to bed; and now, boys, come and let us dance the Horo Lheig in the barn hideout.

But you see, boys, before we go, and in order that I may make everything plain, I better tell you that Harry, in crossing the bridge of Ballyboulteen, a couple of miles below Squire Bragshaw's demense-wall, saw the pudding floating down the river - the truth is he was waiting for it; but be this as it may, he took it out, for the weather had made it as clean as a new pin, and tucking it up in the tail of his big coat, contrived, as you all guess, I suppose, to change it while Paddy Scanlan and the wife were examining the sky; and for the other, he contrived to bewitch it in the same manner, by getting a fairy to go into it, for, indeed, it was pretty well known that the same Harry was hand and glove with the good people. Others will tell you that it was half a pound of quicksilver he put into it; but that doesn't stand to reason.

At any rate, boys and girls, I've told you the adventures of the Mad Pudding of Ballyboulteen; but I don't wish to tell you many other things about it that happened—in case I'd tell a lie."

Rathlin, The Enchanted Island
Anonymous

To Rathlin's Isle I chanced to sail,
When summer breezes softly blew,
And there I heard so sweet a tale,
That oft I wished it could be true.
They said, at eve, when rude winds sleep,
And hushed is every turbid swell,
A mermaid rises from the deep,
And sweetly tunes her magic shell.

And while she plays, rock, dell, and cave
In dying falls the sound retain,
As if some choral spirits gave
Their aid to swell her witching strain.
Then summoned by that dulcet note,
Uprising to the admiring view,
A fairy island seems to float
With tints of many a gorgeous hue.

And glittering fanes and lofty towers
All on this fairy isle are seen;
And waving trees and shady bowers,
With more than mortal verdure green.
And as it moves, the western sky
Glows with a thousand varying rays;
And the calm sea, tinged with each dye,
Seems like a golden flood of blaze.

They also say, if earth or stone
From verdant Erin's hallowed land
Were on this magic island thrown,
Forever fixed it then would stand.
But when for this some little boat
In silence ventures from the shore,
The mermaid sinks, hushed is the note,
The fairy isle is seen no more!

Bibliography & References

Allington, D. (2012) 'Material English', in D.Allington and B.Mayor (eds), *Communicating in English; Talk, Text and Technology,* Abingdon / Milton Keynes, Routledge in association with The Open University, word spacing p.275

Atthill, Dr. Lombe (2015*) Recollections of an Irish Doctor (Glossary Edition)* Analogy Press, Belfast

Barclay, K. (2012) 'Place and Power in Irish Farms at the End of the Nineteenth Century' in *Women's History Review Volume 21, Issue 4* 2012, p573

Bridges, Professor J. Barry *Belfast Medical Students* Department of Physiology, The Queen's University of Belfast, p 37, available at http://www.ums.ac.uk/bmsa/bmsa_med.pdf

Bullock, Shan F. (1912) *Thomas Andrews Shipbuilder, With an Introduction by Sir Horace Plunkett.* Maunsel & Company, Ltd Dublin and London

Carmichael Ferrall, E. (1913) *The Augher Book of Maxims, Household Hints and Recipes* W.G. Baird, Ltd., Royal Avenue, Belfast.

Cust, Henry (2015) *The Poetry of Henry Cust* Analogy Press, Belfast

Daily Mirror April 16th 1912

Daily Mirror April 17th 1912

Graves, Alfred Perceval , Editor (191-?) *The Book of Irish Poetry* Dublin, The Talbot Press

Irish Society and Social Review, Ewart Wedding September 24, 1904

Isobel's Home Cookery Volume 8 (1903)   C. Arthur Pearson Ltd. London

Kander, Lizzie Black (undated) *The Way to a Man's Heart*

McBride, Jack (1983) *Traveller in the Glens* Appletree Press pp 23-25

McFadden, J. , Kiefer, D. et al 'Abstracted in his Dreams' Katharine Tynan's W.B. Yeats in Modern Philology Vol. 88 No. 3 (Feb. 1991) The University of Chicago Press p 261

McKnight, Dr William James (1917) *Jefferson County, Pennsylvania - Her Pioneers and People, Vol. II*   J.H. Beers & Company, Chicago, p 654

McSorley, Patricia (1989) *A While With Your Own Ones* Eskra History & Folklore Group. Francis Gervais records p15

Nesbit, E. (September 1901) The High Born Babe in *The Wouldbegoods* pp161, 162, Harper + Brothers Publishers, New York and London

O'Shaughnessey, A. (1874) *Music and Moonlight: Poems and Songs* Chatto and Windus, London

Q.C.B. Cookery Book, compiled in connection with Queen's College Fête, Belfast. (May 1907)

Ricketts, Harry (2000) *Rudyard Kipling: A Life.* Carroll & Graf Publishers Inc.

Sweeney, Patrick (2010) *Liffey Ships and Shipbuilding,* The Mercier Press Ltd. James Maxton, p 146

The Gas World Yearbook Weekly, 1904 & 1914

Tynan, Katharine (1911) *Peeps at Many Lands: Ireland* Adam & Charles Black, London

Maitland, F. and Tynan, K. (1909) *The Book of Flowers* John Murray, London

United States (1901) *Report of the Industrial Commission on the Relations and Conditions of Capital and Labour employed in Manufactures and General Business including testimony so far as taken November 1 1900 and Digest of Testimony.* Volume VII of the Commission's Reports. Washington Government Printing Office.

Urquhart, Diane (2007) *The Ladies of Londonderry: Women and Political Patronage* (International Library of Historical Studies) pp 83 – 84

Waters, O.D.P. (1988) John Boyle O'Reilly in *Seanchas Ardmhacha: Journal of the Armagh Diocesan Historical Society Vol. 13, No. 1* pp. 173 - 184. Cumann Seanchais Ard Mhacha / Armagh Diocesan Historical Society

Yeats, W.B. (1888) *Fairy & Folk Tales of the Irish Peasantry* The Walter Scott Publishing Co. Ltd

Yeats, W.B. (1902) *The Celtic Twilight* A.H. Bullen, London

Yeats, W.B. (1903) *Ideas of Good and Evil* A.H. Bullen, London

Websites:

www.thepeerage.com

"Dr. John Benjamin Story" Online: http://lordbelmontinnorthernireland.blogspot.co.uk/2013/01/corick-house.html (Accessed 27 December 2013)

Cavan fire 1907 Papers Past New Zealand Tablet >23 May 1907 > Page 27 > Irish News found at http://paperspast.natlib.govt.nz/cgi-bin/paperspast?a=d&d=NZT19070523.2.49 (Accessed 30.11.2013)

Connswater Community Greenway website, section D2, Connswater link bridge to Newtownards Road, found at http://www.communitygreenway.co.uk/section-d2/connswater-river-section-2-connswater-link-bridge-to-newtownards-road (Accessed 01.03.2014)

Emily Davison, found at http://www.theguardian.com/society/2013/may/26/emily-davison-suffragette-death-derby-1913

Enhanced British Parliamentary Papers on Ireland "The Report of the President of Queen's College, Belfast for 1907-1908" found at http://eppi.dippam.ac.uk/documents/21206/eppi_pages/589628 (Accessed 07 November 2013)

Federation of Historical Bottle Collectors website. Ginger Ale's Irish Roots by Ken Previtali (2003)
http://www.fohbc.org/PDF_Files/GingerAle_Previtali.pdf
(Accessed 17 February 2014)

Nottinghamshire History, Coombs' Eureka Aerated Flour Co., Ltd. Found at http://www.nottshistory.org.uk/monographs/nottingham1902/nottingham24.htm (Accessed 24 January 2014)

London Gazette 14 December 1909, found at
https://www.thegazette.co.uk/London/issue/28317/page/9536

London Gazette 15 August 1913, found at
https://www.thegazette.co.uk/London/issue/28746/page/5884

Oxford Index "Lady Theresa Susey Helen Chetwynd-Talbot" found at http://www.oxforddnb.com/templates/article.jsp?articleid=36626&back= (Accessed 21 December 2013)

Princess Victoria sinking http://www.express.co.uk/news/uk/370401/The-maritime-tragedy-that-Scotland-forgot

"Scot " Encyclopædia Britannica Online. Retrieved 10 March, 2014 from http://www.britannica.com/EBchecked/topic/529398/Scot

"Scot", Online Etymology Dictionary. Retrieved 10 March 2014 from http://www.etymonline.com/index.php?term=Scot

Sir Ivan Ewart biography – Ulster History Circle, Dictionary of Ulster Biography (online) found at http://www.newulsterbiography.co.uk/index.php/home/viewPerson/1798

Thornton, M. (2013) http://www.express.co.uk/news/uk/393503/Did-True-Blue-blood-run-in-Lady-Thatcher-s-veins

"Tilly the Tomboy visits the Poor" (1910) Online, BFI National Archive, at http://www.youtube.com/watch?v=5UqR8iiN6iw

The Wreck of the "Ceres" 1866. A survivor's story (online) found at http://www.coastguardsofyesteryear.org/articles.php?article_id=191 (Accessed 30 November 2013)

United States Census Bureau *Immigration by Country of Origin: 1901 -1949* found at http://www2.census.gov/prod2/statcomp/documents/1950-03.pdf

Wilson, John -The Thoroton Society of Nottinghamshire – "Coombs' 'Eureka' Aerated Flour Company Ltd – A Nottingham business found at http://www.thorotonsociety.org.uk/publications/articles/coombs.htm (Accessed 01.01.2014)

Wreck of The Ceres, Irish Shipwrecks Website, found at http://www.irishshipwrecks.com/shipwrecks.php?wreck_ref=393 (Accessed 07 January 2014)

People & Places Index

Andrews, Thomas,   22, 70, 71, 73
Anderson and McAuley,   156
Atthill, Dr. Lombe,   11, 29, 30, 31
Augher Castle,   117
Beckenham,   20
Belfast Ropeworks Co.,   156
Bloomfield bakery,   142
Bretland, Josiah,   93
Bretland, Maria,   93, 94
Bretland, Norah Madeline,   94
Burges, Mrs Ynyr,   130
Carmichael Ferrall, Elizabeth,   103
Carmichael Ferrall, John,   103
Carmichael Ferrall, Captain John Jervis O'Ferrall,   103
Carmichael, Sir Hugh Lyle,   103
Cabinet Pudding,   146
Canada, labour demand,   155
Cecil Manor, Clogher,   149
Ceres, Wreck of the,   108
Churchill, Winston,   64
Coombs' Eureka Aerated Flour Company,   88, 97, 121
Cooper, William,   13
Corick House, Clogher,   147
Cust, Harry / Henry,   63, 68, 69
Drew, Cherry,   103
Drew, Henry,   103
Donaghadee, Co Down,   108
East Bread Street, Belfast,   137, 142
Eiffel Tower Lemonade,   91, 92
Ewart, Fred,   85, 86
Ewart, Sir William,   20
Ewart, Violet Villiers,   20, 85
Garron Tower,   64
Gervais, Dorothy,   146, 147

Gervais, Francis Peter, 149
Goethe, Johann Wolfgang von, 90, 127
Grattan & Co. Ltd., 148
Grattan's Fruit Cordials, 148
Gullan, Hector Freeman, 77
Gullan, Laura Beatriz, 77, 78
Hamilton, Edward Vicars, Omagh, 127
Healy, Patrick, 103
Heard, Dr. Robert Lynn, 108
Heard, Emily Elizabeth Maude, 108
Heard, Richard Griffith Noble, 108
Jaffe, Lady, 21
Jaffe, Sir Otto, 21
Jerome, Jennie, 64
Londonderry Air, 159
Londonderry, Lady, 63
Londonderry, Lord, 63
Louis heels, 160
Lutwyche, Gerald, 20
Maeterlinck, Maurice, 64
Marvin, Joan, 153
Maxton, James, 64
Maxton, Mary Edwards, 64
Maze, restaurant, Belfast, 22
McGrath, Sean, 19
McWatter's bakery, 156
Megahy's bakery, 156
"Mexican Hearts Aflame", 153
Millwall F.C., 97
Milroy, Mrs, 92
Mocollup Castle, 103
Montgomery, Alexander, 117
Nesselrode Pudding, 57, 60
Naylor's bakery, 156
Northern Whig, 158
Nottingham Forest F.C., 97

Nottingham Goose Fair, 97
Ormeau bakery, 156
O'Reilly, John Boyle, 44, 58
O'Shaughnessy, A., 16
Princess Victoria sinking, 142
Pot Pourri, 52
Rheumatism Remedy, 118
Robinson and Cleaver, 160
Rossmore, Lord, Cavan, 61
Ross's bakery, 156
Royal Arms Hotel, 19
Rhyde, Thomas, 153
Studebaker cars, 156
Sweet Scented Bags to lay with Linen, 52
Synge, John Millington, 96
Turnley, Francis, 64
Tynan, Katharine, 50 - 52, 54, 56, 159
Van der Berg, Antge, 103
Vane, Frances Anne, Marchioness of Londonderry, 64
Wouldbegoods, the, 92
Wreck of the Ceres, 108
White, Maria Elizabeth, 93, 94
Whitla, Lady, 63, 85
Whitla, Sir William, 85

Recipe Index

A
An Apple Hedgehog, 104
American Fruit or Wedding Cake, 182
Apple Amber Pudding, 102
Apple, Celery & Nut Salad (Waldorf), 172
Apple Sponge Pudding, 48
Apple Strudel, 180
Apple Tart, thick pastry, 49
Apple Tart Pastry, thin, 71
Autumn Jelly, 54

B
Banana Pudding, 114
Blackberry Cake, 55
Blackberry or Elderberry Cordial, 185
Blackstone Salad Dressing, 173
Boiled Mayonnaise Sauce, 80
Border of Rice with Plums, 37
Buttermilk Oaten Bread, 35
Buttermilk Soda Bread, 166

C
Cabbage with Sausage, 84
Carrageen Moss Jelly, 116
Cherry Cake, 108
Chocolate Cake, 111
Chocolate Icing, 112
Chocolate Syrup, 184
Chicken and Ham Pie Filling, 86
Chutney, 130
Christmas Crumble, 28
Christmas Pudding, 25
Cinnamon Biscuits, 106
Clover Leaf Tea Rolls, 168
Club Sandwiches, 171

Cocoa Bread, 166
Cod Curry, 80
Cranberry Relish, raw, 175
Cressy or French Carrot Soup, 110
Curried Eggs, 75
Custard Sauce, 181

D
Dairy- Free Fadge Soda Bread, 34
Dandelion Punch, 185
Duchess Pudding, 117

E
Eel Pie, 99
Elderberry Cordial, 185

F
Fish Gateau, 79
Fish Pâtés, 77
French Pastry for Chocolate Painted Éclairs, 88
Fresh Milk Wheaten Bread Recipe, 41
French Toast, 169
Fried Tomatoes, 58
Frog Legs, 178
Frozen Fruit Cubes, 187
Fruit Compote, 87
Fruit Squares, 83

G
Gaelic Steak, 59
German Biscuits, 92
Ginger Sponge Squares, 60
Gooseberry & Almond Tartlets, 101
Green Pepper Butter, 170
Green Sauce, 131

H
Harvey's Sauce, 100

I
Ice Cubes, decorative, 187
Icing for Coconut Sandwich Cake, 123
Irish Oatcakes, 116

K
Kedgeree, 131

L
Lobster Cream, 78

M
Marrow Marmalade, 128
Melba Toast, 169
Mixed Spice, 144
Mushroom Pie, 120
Mustard for the Table, 179
Mysterious Pudding, 145

O
Oaten Apple, 31
O'Brien Potatoes, 179
Oaten Honeycomb, 65
Old Irish Buutermilk Cheesecake, 61
Open Faced Sandwiches, 175
Orange & Blackberry Pudding, 53
Oysters Au Gratin, 176
Oysters, Fried, 176
Oysters in Blankets, 177
Oysters Manhattan Style, 177

P
Pancakes, 23

Pancakes, Whiskey, 82
Parker House Rolls, 167
Peanut Butter Bread, 167
Pimento Butter, 170
Pineapple Pudding, 18
Pineapple Punch, 184
Plum Cake, 94
Potato Apple, 152
Potato Bread, 57
Potatoes, Creamed, 68
Potato Pudding, 151
Potato Salad, warm, 172

R
Raspberry Jam, 65
Red Pottage, 157
Rhubarb Crumble, 44
Rhubarb Jam, 109
Rousham's Royal Bengal Chutney, 93
Rinktum Dity, 174

S
Sandwich Cake, 112
Sardine & Cucumber Sandwiches, 171
Savoury Rice Cutlets, 147
Scrambled Egg Sandwich, 175
Soda Bread, brown, 75
Soda Bread, spicy fruit, 38
Soubise Soup, 66
Sponge Cake, 124
Steamed Rhubarb, 106
Strawberry or Raspberry Whip, 104
Stuffed Dates, 183
Stuffed Sausages, 47
Sultana Scones, 33
Summer Fruits Jam, 46

Sunshine Punch, 187

T
Teabread, 45
Tea Punch, 186
Thousand Island Dressing, 174
Toast Points, 169
Tomato & Egg Scramble, 64
Tomato Open Faced Sandwiches, 170

V
Vinegar Pastry, 85
Vol au Vent of Custard, 154

W
Waldorf Salad, 172
Warm Potato Salad, 172
Watercress Open Faced Sandwiches, 171
Wheaten Bread, Milk, 41

Printed in Great Britain
by Amazon.co.uk, Ltd.,
Marston Gate.